CAMPAIGN 415

THE JUGURTHINE WAR 112–106 BC

Rome's Long War in North Africa

NIC FIELDS   ILLUSTRATED BY MARCO CAPPARONI

OSPREY PUBLISHING
Bloomsbury Publishing Plc
Kemp House, Chawley Park, Cumnor Hill, Oxford OX2 9PH, UK
Bloomsbury Publishing Ireland Limited,
29 Earlsfort Terrace, Dublin 2, D02 AY28, Ireland
1385 Broadway, 5th Floor, New York, NY 10018, USA
E-mail: info@ospreypublishing.com
www.ospreypublishing.com

OSPREY is a trademark of Osprey Publishing Ltd

First published in Great Britain in 2025

© Osprey Publishing Ltd, 2025

All rights reserved. No part of this publication may be: i) reproduced or transmitted in any form, electronic or mechanical, including photocopying, recording or by means of any information storage or retrieval system without prior permission in writing from the publishers; or ii) used or reproduced in any way for the training, development or operation of artificial intelligence (AI) technologies, including generative AI technologies. The rights holders expressly reserve this publication from the text and data mining exception as per Article 4(3) of the Digital Single Market Directive (EU) 2019/790

A catalogue record for this book is available from the British Library.

ISBN: PB 9781472865465; eBook 9781472865472; ePDF 9781472865489; XML 9781472865496

25 26 27 28 29   10 9 8 7 6 5 4 3 2 1

Maps by Bounford.com
3D BEVs by Paul Kime
Index by Fionbar Lyons
Typeset by PDQ Digital Media Solutions, Bungay, UK
Printed by Repro India Ltd.

MIX Paper FSC® C047271

Osprey Publishing supports the Woodland Trust, the UK's leading woodland conservation charity.

To find out more about our authors and books visit www.ospreypublishing.com. Here you will find extracts, author interviews, details of forthcoming events and the option to sign up for our newsletter.

For product safety related questions contact productsafety@bloomsbury.com

Abbreviations

Ael.	Aelianus, *De natura animalium*
App.	Appianus
B civ.	*Bellum civilia*
Iber.	*Ibērikē*
Num.	*Nomantinōn polemon*
Pun.	*Libykē*
Appul.	Appuleius, *Apologia*
Ascon.	Asconius
B Cat.	Sallust, *Bellum Catilinae*
B Iug.	Sallust, *Bellum Iugurthinum*
Caes.	Caesar
B Afr.	*Bellum Africum*
B civ.	*Bellum civile*
Cic.	Cicero
Att.	*Epistulae ad Atticus*
Brut.	*Brutus*
Leg.	*Leges*
Orat.	*De oratore*
Rep.	*De re publica*
Tusc.	*Tusculanae disputationes*
CIL	T. Mommsen et al., *Corpus Inscriptionum Latinarum* (Berlin, 1863–)
cos.	consul
Dio	Cassius Dio
Diod.	Diodoros Sikoulos, *Bibliothēkē*
Eutr.	Eutropios, *Breviarium*
Fest.	Sextus Pompeius Festus, *Glossaria Latina*
Flor.	Lucius Annaeus Florus, *Epitomae de Tito Livio*
Frontin.	Frontinus, *Strategemata*
Gell.	Aulus Gellius, *Noctes Atticae*
Gk.	Greek
Inst. or	Quintilianus, *Institutio oratoria*
Just.	Justinus, *Epitome* (of Cnaeus Pompeius Trogus)
KAI	H. Donner and W. Röllig, *Kanaanäische und Aramäische Inschriften*, 3 vols (Wiesbaden, 1962–64)
L	Latin
Liv.	Livy, *Ab urbe condita* ('History of Rome')
Per.	*Periochae* ('Epitome')
Luc.	Lucan, *Pharsalia* (*De Bello Civili*)
Oros.	Orosius, *Historiarum adversus paganos libri VII*
Plin.	Pliny the Elder, *Naturalis historia*
Plut.	Plutarch
C. Gracch.	*Caius Gracchus*
Cat. mai.	*Cato maior*
Lucull.	*Lucullus*
Mar.	*Caius Marius*
Pyrr.	*Pyrrhos*
Sull.	*Sulla*
Polyain.	Polyainos, *Strategemata*
Polyb.	Polybios
RIL	J.-B. Chabot, *Recueil des inscriptions libyques* (Paris, 1940)
RRC	M. H. Crawford, *Roman Republican Coinage*, 2 vols (Cambridge, 1974)
Sil.	Silius Italicus, *Punica*
Strab.	Strabo, *Geographia*
Tac.	Tacitus
Agr.	*Agricola*
Ann.	*Annales*
Hist.	*Historiae*
Val. Max.	Valerius Maximus, *Factotem et dictorem memoribilius*
Veg.	Vegetius, *Epitoma rei militaris*
Vell.	Velleius Paterculus, *Historiae Romanae*
Ver.	Virgil, *Aeneid*
Vir. ill.	Anon., *De viris illustribus*

Front cover main illustration: Ignominious capitulation of Aulus Postumius Albinus. (Marco Capparoni)
Title page photograph: Numidian horsemen fighting Dacians. (Benjamín Núñez González, CC BY-SA 4.0 https://creativecommons.org/licenses/by-sa/4.0, via Wikimedia Commons)

CONTENTS

INTRODUCTION 5

CHRONOLOGY 11

OPPOSING COMMANDERS 12
Numidians . Romans

OPPOSING FORCES 21
Numidians . Romans

THE CAMPAIGN 42
Family drama . Cousins' war . Bestia takes command . Spurius Postumius takes command
Metellus takes command . Marius takes command . Sallust's distant, dirty war

AFTERMATH 88

FURTHER READING 92

INDEX 95

North Africa at the time of the Jugurthine War

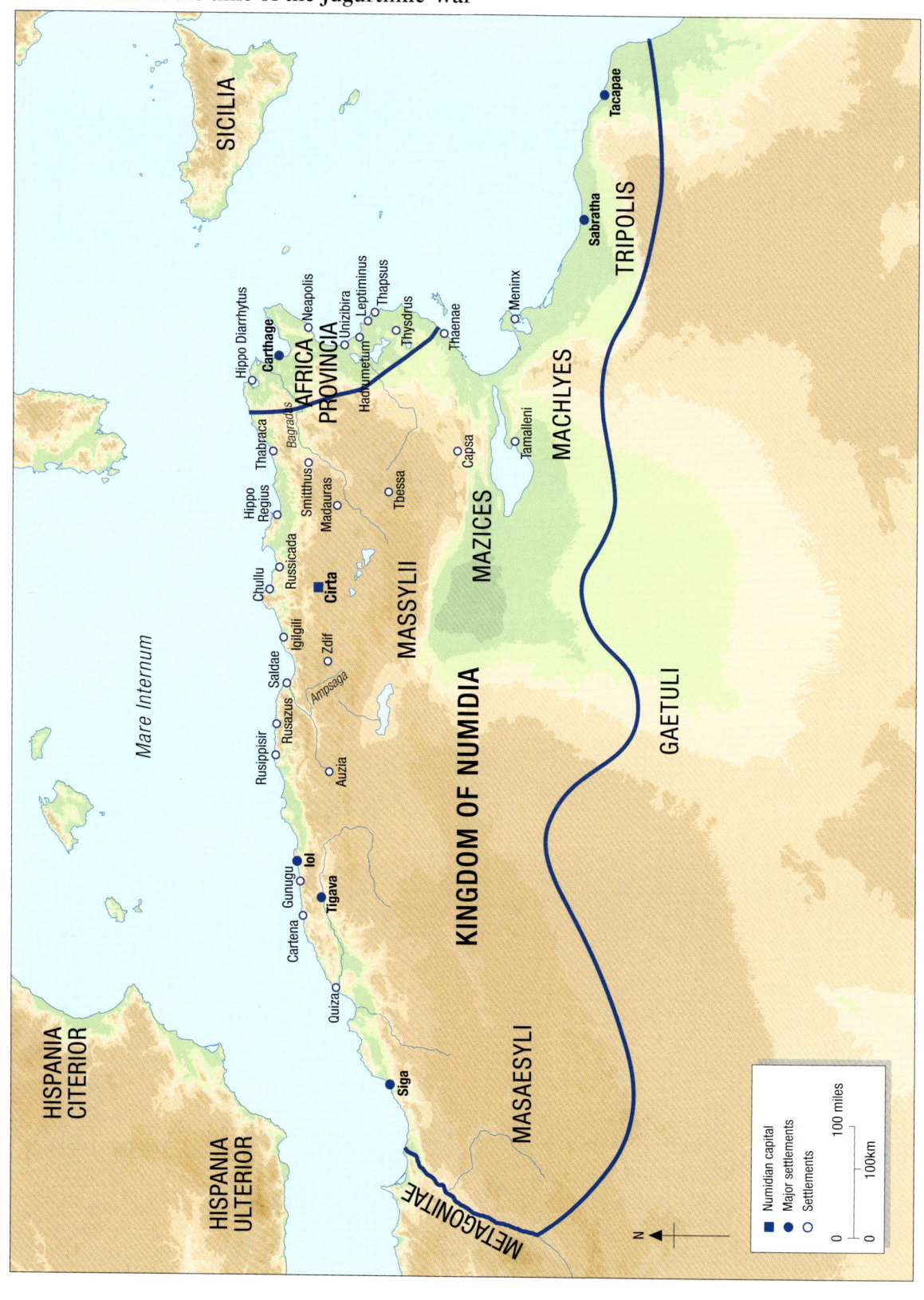

INTRODUCTION

Beneath whose awful hand we hold / Dominion over palm and pine
Rudyard Kipling, 'Recessional', 1.3–4[1]

It has been said in certain military quarters that amateurs talk about tactics whereas professionals study logistics. This is correct, and they rightly regard logistics as a principle of war. '[A]rmies are more often destroyed by starvation than battle,' Vegetius once ruefully reflected, 'and hunger is more savage than the sword' (3.3, cf. Frontin. 4.7.1, Caes. *B civ*. 1.72.1). The Roman Army, which relied on heavily equipped, close-ordered disciplined infantry, was no exception to this stark truth. As such, it was best suited for high-intensity warfare against a dense agricultural population with conquerable assets. It was less well suited for mobile warfare against lightly equipped, mobile opponents. It also needed to be well rested, fed and equipped. For these reasons, though it was an apex expansionist predator, Rome would settle for what its army could handle and its agriculturists could exploit, and so the policy of imperial expansion excluded any designs on the steppe, the forest and the desert. Ideally, this meant ruling out the expanse of Eurasia, northern European lands such as Germania and Britannia,[2] and Africa south of the Mediterranean littoral. It would be in the semi-desert of the latter arena that the Romans would face the Numidians, in an unforgiving landscape that was suitable to the brilliant feats of horsemanship on which the strength of these people was based.

Numidia was a kingdom on the north coast of Africa. From the earliest times, northern Africa, through the medium of trade and of warfare, has represented an area of contact between agonistic empires. The Romans first came to this part of the world in 256 BC when Marcus Atilius Regulus and his consular army landed on a beach somewhere near Utica. His exploits on African soil were short lived and, for him at least, tragic, suffering a fate rather more gruesome than merely losing a battle. Almost exactly half a century later, in 204 BC, Publius Cornelius Scipio mounted a full-scale invasion of Carthaginian territory, and his forces, two years on, would face and defeat one of history's greatest generals, Hannibal Barca. The victory in Africa rightly earned him a triumph and the cognomen *Africanus*. Still, the creation of the province of Africa would have to wait until 146 BC following

---

1 First published in *The Times* on 17 July 1897, reprinted in *The Spectator* on 24 July 1897.
2 In a passage concerning Britannia, Strabo (4.5.3) explains why it was useless to conquer lands with poor resources, that is to say, keeping them would soon outstrip any economic benefits. The geographer was writing in the age of Augustus and of course we are faced with the ironic fact that the Claudian invasion of AD 43, and the campaigns that followed, meant the Romans nevertheless occupied a large chunk of Britannia.

Rome's destruction of Carthage: the elder Cato (234–149 BC), an embattled idealist, had conjured up a wounded, vengeful Carthage that remained a threat as long as it existed.

Maps of the Roman Empire habitually show frontiers clearly marked with thick black lines. Perceptibly, these lines of territorial confines offer the viewer the marked feeling that if you were on one side of a particular line you were inside, and if you were on the opposite side, you were outside. The reality of course was not that simple. There were *provinciae* (provinces) for which the Romans accepted some degree of administrative responsibility (the bare minimum in the period we are concerned with), and to which the Senate sent a governor (either a *pro praetore* or a *pro consule*) and in some cases a handful of garrison troops. But beyond the *provinciae*, the Romans were at pains to make alliances with local powers, so as to secure their loyalty or at least their compliance. The doubtful policy of setting up puppet rulers unfortunately meant the men were all too often puppets in nature as well as name.

Still, the Romans, always ready to concede the appearance of power as long as they held the reality, awarded those who made such alliances with Rome the simple title of *amicus* (friend), or sometimes *socius et amicus* (ally and friend), or more impressive still, *socius et amicus populi Romani* (ally and friend of the Roman people). Naturally, no matter the actual title awarded by the Senate, the honourable diplomatic relationship gradually transformed independent rulers into clients of Rome.

The geopolitical aspect of northern Africa at the start of the Jugurthine War was essentially quadripartite. In 146 BC, at the conclusion of the third and final war with Carthage, Rome had annexed Carthage's territories, creating *provincia Africa* with its capital at Utica (Utique, Tunisia). This left to the king of the Numidians much of the land Masinissa (r. 202–148 BC) had appropriated from the Carthaginians as well as his own kingdom, today's western Tunisia and eastern Algeria.

To the west, in what the Romans knew as Mauretania, today's western Algeria and northern Morocco, was found the kingdom of Bocchus I, a name that was to become black in treachery. Mauretanians (possibly from the Phoenician *Mahurin*, meaning 'Westerners') had loyally served with Hannibal Barca in the Italian peninsula, both horse and foot (Liv. 22.37.8, 24.15.3, 20.16). We know of an alliance in the 4th century BC and again around 150 BC (Just. 21.4.7, Polyb. 38.7.9, App. *Pun.* 16 §111). We also know that in 406 BC the Carthaginian army that came ashore in Sicilia had included Mauretanians (and Numidians) 'who were their allies' (Diod. 13.80.3). Ethnically speaking, they were of the same racial origins as the Numidians, and Polybios evidently regarded these ancestral cousins as one and the same. In fact, during the Second Punic War (218–201 BC), the Mauretanian tribes formed a confederacy under a king called Baga, and appear not to have had any formal relationship with Carthage at this time (Law 1978: 188). The Mauretanians deployed in Hannibal's first line at Zama (202 BC) were mercenaries (Polyb. 15.11.1).

The fourth and final part of the African jigsaw consisted of a long band along the pre-desert, on and south of the Atlas Mountains, which separate the Sahara Desert from the Mediterranean Sea and the Atlantic Ocean. Here, in what was a rugged hostile territory of climate extremes, the Gaetulians eked out a contented if challenging existence, a cluster of tribes who lay

Roman Empire, mid-2nd century BC

Oued Rhumel, the ancient Ampsaga, at its source in the Ferdjioua mountains, north-eastern Algeria. In pre-Roman times, this river formed the boundary between the two Numidian tribal confederations, the Massylii to the east and the Masaesyli to the west. When the more prosperous eastern part was annexed in 46 BC by Caesar, the lower course of the Ampsaga became the western boundary of Africa Nova. This new province he put into the hands of Sallust. (Mouhieddine Kherouatou, CC BY-SA 4.0 https://creativecommons.org/licenses/by-sa/4.0, via Wikimedia Commons)

outside the two kingdoms of Numidia and Mauretania and resisted any attempts to tax or control them (Strab. 17.3.9, cf. [Caes.] *B Afr.* 25.2, Appul. 24.1). The Gaetulians, like the Mauretanians, were of the same racial group as the Numidians. Roman references to them suggest Gaetulian horsemen, like their Numidian cousins, lacked bridles (e.g. [Caes.] *B Afr.* 32, 56, 61). It is assumed they were armed and fought in the same fashion too, which would explain why Polybios, for instance, never mentions them. In a barbed comment, Sallust describes them as 'rough and uncivilized folk, whose food was the flesh of wild animals and fodder of the ground, like cattle's' (*B Iug.* 18.1, cf. Dio 53.26.2). Much like most folks living on the fringes of so-called civilization, the Gaetulians were resiliently thriving in difficult conditions.

The Numidians (Gk. Νομάδες, L *Numidae*) were part of the northern African cultural group now known as the Berbers or Kabyles, who are found in many of the rugged mountain valleys and desert regions of Morocco and Algiers, and whose language is spoken by the Tuaregs and is found throughout the Sahara as far as Niger, Mali and Burkina Faso. The Numidians were African, but shared the physical characteristics of other Mediterranean populations such as those from Spain or Sicily, rather than those from sub-Saharan Africa or the Levant (Brett and Fentress 1997: 4).

Numidia enters into the full daylight of recorded history during the Second Punic War (218–201 BC). The Numidians were originally nomadic herdsmen, pastoralists who sometimes grew crops. As the elder Pliny says: '[T]he Numidians received their name of Νομάδες from their frequent changes of pasturage; upon which occasions they were accustomed to carry their *mapalia*, or in other words, their houses, upon wagons' (Plin. 5.2).

Livy, referring to the winter quarters of the Carthaginian army outside Utica, provides a little more information concerning the likely fabric of these *mapalia*, for he reports that the Numidians were living in 'huts formed of interwoven reeds, and covered with grass matting' (30.3.9). As for their shape, Sallust says *mapalia* were 'oblong shelters with curved sides, like the hulls of ships' (*B Iug.* 18.8). Normally not a perspicacious observer when it came to ethnological details, this description by Sallust, however, looks like autopsy.

Those Numidians on the coast came under the influence of Carthage and, by the time of the Second Punic War, their small clans, consisting of several agnatic kinship groups, had coalesced into two main tribal confederacies. One was the Massylii under Masinissa (r. 206–202 BC), who lived between the Tusca and the Ampsaga (Rhumel) rivers, and the much larger Masaesyli, ruled by Syphax (r. 215–203 BC), the more westerly of the two, occupying what is now western Algeria north of the Sahara.

During the initial stages of the war, Syphax had been friendly to the Romans. So much so that at one point, a centurion, Quintus Statorius, was outsourced by Rome to organize Syphax's tribal army more or less in the Roman manner, which the king used with success against the Carthaginians (Liv. 24.48.9–12, cf. 30.11.4). Yet Syphax was to ally himself to Carthage when offered Sophonisba, daughter of Hasdrubal Gisgo, in marriage: until 206 BC, she had been betrothed to Masinissa. Conversely, for much of the war, Masinissa had aided the Carthaginians, for instance serving in Hispania with a large body of Numidian horse against the Romans, but later switched sides upon concluding Rome would prevail (Liv. 28.16.35). It is assumed that at the end of the war, Masinissa (202–148 BC, *rex Numidarum*: *B Iug*. 5.4) was given the territory of Syphax in addition to his own (Liv. 30.44.12, cf. 31.11.12). This united Numidia was a reward for his services to Rome: as an ally of Rome, he and his horsemen had played a decisive role in the defeat of Hannibal Barca at Zama (Polyb. 15.5.12, 14.7).

If so, then Jugurtha's Numidia extended as far as the Muluccha (Moulouya) River; Sallust's references to the Muluccha as the frontier of Mauretania appear to confirm this. Yet Livy reports that Syphax, who had died a prisoner at Tibur (Tivoli), was succeeded on the throne by his son Vermina, who had likewise participated in the war. Vermina maintained a small kingdom around modern Oran, north-western Algeria, and sought friendship with Rome (Liv. 31.11.13–17, App. *Pun*. 6 §33). Additionally, a grandson of Syphax, Arcobarzanes, was aiding Carthage against Masinissa at the head of a large Numidian army in 154 BC (*ingens Numidarum exercitus*: Liv. *Per*. 48.4). So Masinissa cannot have ruled Numidia in its totality. Besides, there were also many small, independent tribes with their own chieftains and domains. Pliny (5.1.1–21) alleges some 463 tribes gave allegiance to Rome, though 'Pliny's numerous tribes contain no individuals, and take no actions' (Fentress 1979: 44). Numidian horsemen were formidable and well respected by the Romans, but disunion made them difficult allies politically.

When the young Masinissa began his attempt to regain his father's kingdom, having been driven out by Syphax, 'from farms and villages [*ex agris vicisque*] on all sides old soldiers of Gaïa [his father, †207 BC] flocked to him' (Liv. 29.30.7). Under Masinissa, the timeless world of pastoralism would largely be abandoned, at least in the eastern, coastal part of his kingdom, for mixed agriculture (Strab. 17.3.15, cf. Polyb. 12.3.4). He did so by introducing modern agricultural techniques learned from Carthage, while forcing many Numidians to toil as peasant farmers. Still, the separation between pastoralists and agriculturalists should not be seen as absolute: pastoralists could grow crops and agriculturalists also possessed flocks and herds, and Strabo (17.3.15) mentions that Numidia was well known as a producer of wool. Equally, the elder Pliny reports that 'A small way inland there are no cities, and the normal habitation is a hut. Life is hard …Hunting game is preferred to slaughtering flocks for food. Further inland still the land

Numidian bronze coin (Constantine, Musée national Cirta). Obverse: bust of Masinissa, 202–148 BC. The pro-Roman Numidian king was determined to turn his new kingdom into a modern Mediterranean state and in the course of doing so to expand his boundaries at the expense of Carthage. To Carthage, Masinissa was an opportunist and a criminal. It therefore began to build up military forces, but for defence against Masinissa and not for a war with Rome. A more truculent Carthage emerged, which led to the reiterated demand of the elder Cato that Carthage must be destroyed. And so it was. (Jona Lendering/Livius.org/CC0 1.0 Universal)

Mausoleum of Ateban, Thugga, Tunisia. A contemporary of Masinissa, Ateban was a Numidian chief. Some have conjectured that this Libyco-Punic mausoleum was actually built for Masinissa, who in 202 BC became king of the united Numidian tribes and used Thugga as a royal residence. A limestone frieze with bilingual script (currently in the British Museum) was added to the podium of the mausoleum, the first half of the inscription in Punic, and the second half in Numidian. The inscription (RIL 2, KAI 101) has allowed scholars to decode the Libyco-Berber script, which was written left to right, in which the Numidian language was written. The Numidian name of Thugga in Libyco-Berber was *TBGG*. (Patrick Giraud, CC BY 3.0 https://creativecommons.org/licenses/by/3.0, via Wikimedia Commons)

is entirely uncultivated, and men live a nomadic existence, setting up huts wherever there is pasture. The only unit is the family' (Plin. 5.8).

Concurrently, Punic was adopted as the language of the ruling elite, minting coins using the Semitic language and characters, while beliefs in certain Numidian circles were also affected, as witnessed in the worship of Baal Hammon, Tanit and Baal Addir, alongside indigenous cults. In many ways, Numidia had been transformed into a kingdom of a large number of farming communities ruled by a bilingual, bicultural court. Under the superficial structure of the Numidian state, however, tribal social structures probably remained strong, while on the fringes of this Libyco-Punic civilization, there seems to be little doubt that Numidians existed as they had existed before.

CHRONOLOGY

The chronology of the Jugurthine War has never been clear because Caius Sallustius Crispus (better known as Sallust), the author of *Bellum Iugurthinum*, did not bother with dates. He confined himself to dramatic and political incidents leaving the facts, details and dates to the Roman commentators; but the work of these commentators has been lost, and all that remains is Sallust's historical monograph, which, while interesting, is inconclusive. The following chronological table is probably not far from the truth, but it is impossible to determine the sequence of events with absolute certainty.

133 BC	Jugurtha returns from Numantine War	109 BC	Quintus Caecilius Metellus takes command in Numidia
120 BC	Jugurtha adopted by Micipsa as joint heir with Adherbal and Hiempsal		Roman garrison installed at Vaga
118 BC	Death of Micipsa; tripartite division of Numidia		Battle at the Muthul
117 BC	Murder of Hiempsal		Unsuccessful siege of Zama
116 BC	Adherbal driven from Numidia; appeals to the Senate		Prosecutions at Rome under *lex Mamilia*
	First Roman commission headed by Lucius Opimius	108 BC	Massacre of Roman garrison at Vaga
			Metellus captures Thala
114 BC	Jugurtha attacks Adherbal		Metellus occupies Cirta
113 BC	Adherbal besieged in Cirta; sends envoys to Rome	107 BC	Death of Bomilcar
112 BC	Second Roman commission (three young senators)		Jugurtha secures help of Bocchus of Mauretania
	Fall of Cirta; murder of Adherbal		Caius Marius takes command in Numidia
	Third Roman commission (senior senators under Marcus Aemilius Scaurus)		Marius captures and razes Capsa
		106 BC	Triumph of Metellus
111 BC	War declared by Rome		Lucius Cornelius Sulla arrives in Numidia
	Campaign of Lucius Calpurnius Bestia; settlement with Jugurtha		Battle at the Muluccha
110 BC	Jugurtha at Rome; murder of Massiva	105 BC	Bocchus' betrayal of Jugurtha to Sulla
	Campaign of Spurius Postumius Albinus		Gauda, Jugurtha's half-brother, installed on Numidian throne
	Campaign and capitulation of Aulus Postumius Albinus	104 BC	Triumph of Marius; execution of Jugurtha
			Marius' second consulship; command against Cimbri and Teutones
			Marian army 'reforms'

OPPOSING COMMANDERS

Unhappy the land where heroes are needed.
Bertolt Brecht, *Leben des Galilei* (1939), sc. 13

NUMIDIANS

Everyone knows the first line of Leo Tolstoy's *Anna Karenina* about unhappy families. Notwithstanding, as with every story concerning kin strife, this one is more complicated than it seems, not least due to time and opinions in the Roman Senate. Rival siblings, a disappointed father, resentful sons, cowards, double-crossers and an elusive anti-hero: the affair known as the Jugurthine War has it all. This intensity of intra-familial hatred was to set in motion a series of events that was to shake the very socio-political fabric of Rome itself.

The long-lived, pro-Roman Masinissa of Numidia had been succeeded upon his death in 148 BC by his three legitimate sons Mastanabal, Gulussa

Reconstructed façade of Numidian monument (Musée de Chemtou), *c.* 130 BC. It was built on the command of Micipsa. The depictions of the shields and the body armour on the marble frieze appear to be in the form of Greek *aspídes* (broad flat-rim, soup-bowl shape) and *linothōraxes* (shoulder pieces, *pteruges*). One of the shields has a Greek-style blazon in the form of an eye (to ward off evil?). The monument was originally adorned with Hellenistic statues. (Carole Raddato, CC BY-SA 2.0 https://creativecommons.org/licenses/by-sa/2.0, via Wikimedia Commons)

and Micipsa (Liv. *Per*. 50.6). Mastanabal and Gulussa soon disappeared from the scene – they mysteriously 'died from illness' (*B Iug*. 5.7) – leaving the last brother as the sole ruler of the kingdom. Mastanabal, however, had a son by a concubine who, because the offspring of concubines were not considered legitimate according to Numidian law, remained a commoner. Nonetheless, he seems to have grown up with all conventionally desired princely traits: an outstanding physique, good looks, intelligence, bravery, skill-at-arms and an all-round athlete, a young warrior with brains and brawn (*B Iug*. 6.1). And he was popular with the people too. The illegitimate boy was **Jugurtha**.

All of this presented Micipsa with some difficulties. He himself had two legitimate sons, Adherbal and Hiempsal, who he naturally wished to see succeed him. He had, however, raised Jugurtha in his royal ménage with the two younger boys, making little distinction between their statuses. Sallust, writing years later, suggests that Jugurtha's princely qualities began to trouble the king, who saw him as a threat to his own beloved offspring, particularly in view of his popularity. Yet it was this popularity with the people, continues Sallust, which protected him from his uncle, who feared rebellion if he discreetly disposed of the young man. So, Micipsa hit upon the idea of making Jugurtha the commander of a Numidian contingent he was about to dispatch to Hispania, as the Romans called the Iberian Peninsula. Once there, the contingent served alongside the Roman forces under Publius Cornelius Scipio Aemilianus (*cos*. 147 BC, *cos*. II 134 BC), the destroyer of Carthage, during the siege of Numantia (134–133 BC). Overseas, and out of the public eye, there would always be a chance that the impetuous young man, who seemed to have found an outlet for his personal frustrations in battlefield aggression, would be killed in action (*B Iug*. 7.2).

The habitually reckless Jugurtha was not only to survive but to serve with individualistic distinction (as did a fellow officer, one Caius Marius). Both 'vigorous in battle and wise in counsel' (*B Iug*. 7.5), it was during the siege that the young prince had earned Scipio Aemilianus' approval by his soldierly qualities, but it also encouraged a Roman belief that their most dangerous opponents were the foreign individuals whom they themselves had taught how to fight. This deep-rooted attitude of racial superiority, coupled with a deficiency in practical application where Numidians were concerned, reveals a Roman disregard for Numidian fighting potential, a pretermission that would come back to haunt the Romans. For the time being, though, Jugurtha was to learn in Hispania the venality of many of the Romans.

Numidian silver *didrakhmon* (Paris, Bibliothèque nationale de France, département Monnaies, inv. Luynes 3960). Obverse: bust of Jugurtha. Well-built and athletic, Jugurtha was an excellent horseman and javelineer. Comfortable with violence, another weapon of choice for Jugurtha was assassination. Once master and loyal ally, Rome and Jugurtha were now bitter foes. Jugurtha knew both the strengths and the weaknesses of the Republic. Sallust portrays him as a gifted but fatally flawed anti-hero. (Public domian, Bibliothèque nationale de France, département Monnaies, médailles et antiques, Luynes.3960 [43-59-39])

Siegeworks around Numantia (134–133 BC): Jugurtha's first contact with the Romans

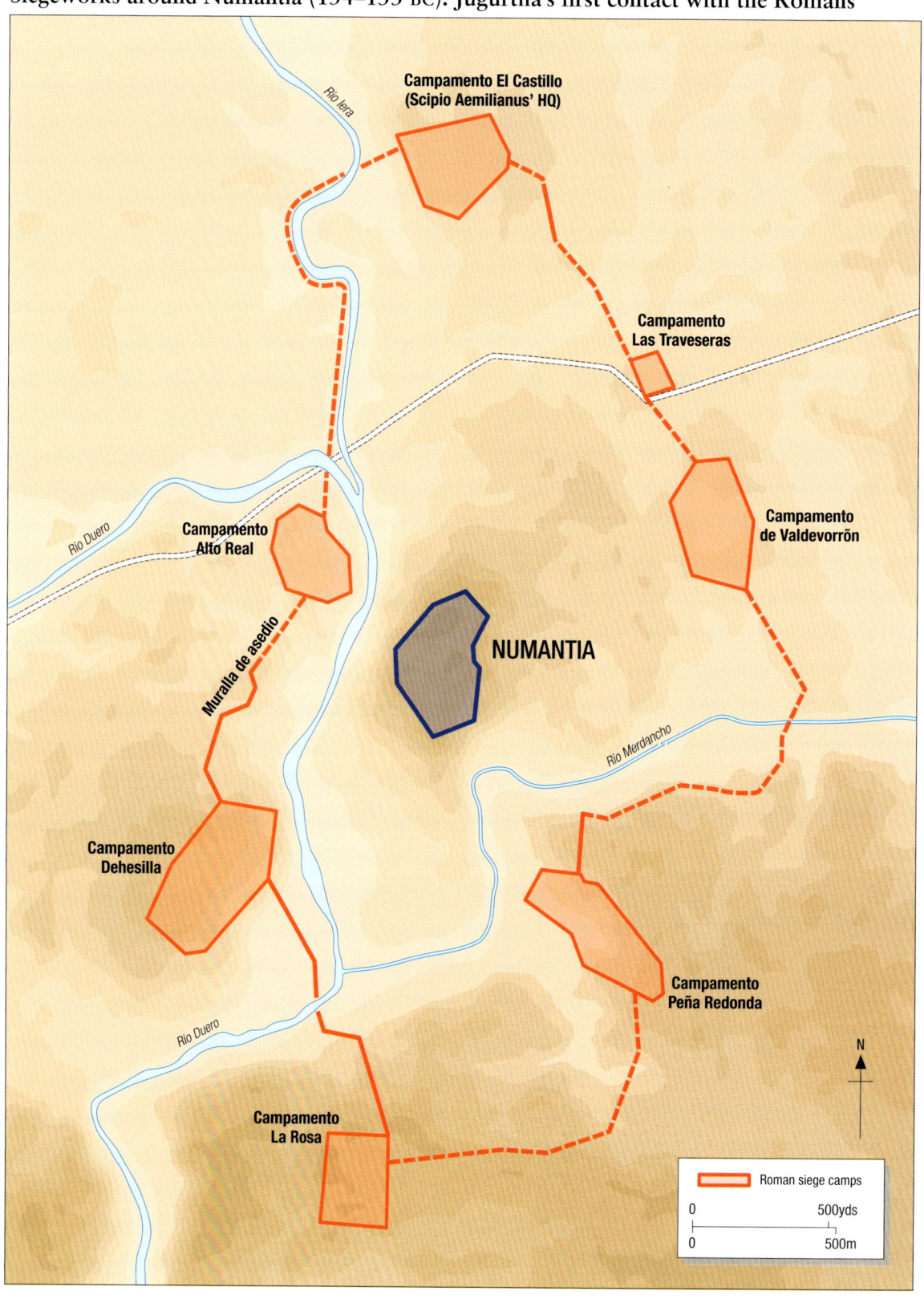

ABOVE LEFT
Historical reenactment of the siege of Numantia (134–133 BC), Garray, near Soria, Castile-León. It was during the siege that Marius and Jugurtha observed a master besieger at work, Publius Cornelius Scipio Aemilianus. The fall of Numantia secured, at last, almost the entire region of the Iberian Peninsula for Rome. (Franciscojhh, CC BY-SA 4.0 https://creativecommons.org/licenses/by-sa/4.0, via Wikimedia Commons)

ABOVE RIGHT
Reconstruction of the Celtiberian defences at the site of Numantia. Numantia was an Iron Age hill fort, what the Romans called an *oppidum*, which controlled a crossing of the upper reaches of the Durius (Douro/Duero) River. Little remains of what were once substantial defensive walls surrounding at least three roughly concentric fortified precincts at different levels, all strengthened by large square towers. (Multitud, CC BY 3.0 https://creativecommons.org/licenses/by/3.0, via Wikimedia Commons)

Intrigue in the Roman siege camps was rife. And so it was that over the course of the campaign, Jugurtha fell in with more unsavoury company, venal and unscrupulous characters that aroused his innate ambitions by urging him to stage a *coup d'état* upon the death of Micipsa and wrest control of Numidia from Adherbal and Hiempsal. It is almost certainly these men that Sallust later calls '*veteres amicos*' (*B Iug*. 13.6, cf. 7.7, 8.1), the very young men (*novi*) Jugurtha had befriended at Numantia, who were to become helpful to him two decades later when they were senators.

At the time, a troubled Scipio Aemilianus got wind of this deplorable plan and warned Jugurtha not to consort with some of Rome's more crooked nobles in order to pursue his own growing ambitions. Scipio Aemilianus also added it was not only dangerous, but stupid, to buy power (*B Iug*. 8.2). Sadly, this sage advice was to fall on deaf ears, and Micipsa's fears were to be justified.

With the destruction of Numantia, Jugurtha was mustered out. He returned home with his reputation greatly burnished. He had operated as part of the Roman Army itself. He had gained a very good understanding of the Roman character, and won useful friends. He had even mastered Latin. Significantly too, he came home bearing a glowing letter of recommendation from Scipio Aemilianus (*B Iug*. 9.1–2). Following his suggestion – which was more or less a command – Micipsa decided to adopt his nephew and include him in a three-way split of the kingdom with his biological sons, both younger than Jugurtha. It was an act of patronage that the Romans later were to regret. True to his nature, Jugurtha would not be content to share with his adopted brothers. In his own mind, Jugurtha believed he was altogether more fit to rule than them, a conviction that meant he was more than willing to take the kingdom from them when the time came. Power, of course, when finally achieved, is addictive, and Jugurtha would prove to be one of the most tenacious enemies of Rome.

With the passing of Micipsa, Jugurtha quickly arranged the assassination of Hiempsal, and went on to initiate a war against Adherbal. Despite the blatant illegitimacy of the usurper's actions, Rome's response was initially hampered by divisions within the Senate, where Jugurtha's envoys had apparently managed to buy off a number of senators. Emboldened by the political and social corruption he saw in Rome, Jugurtha became increasingly dismissive of Rome's resolve to guarantee Adherbal's security, as 'he felt

ABOVE LEFT
Mausoleum Soumaā d'el-Khroub, some 15km south-east of Cirta. What survives is the base of what was once a Punic tower tomb, comparable to the one at Thugga: the needle-like superstructure has long disappeared. The presence of late 2nd century BC Rhodian amphorae suggests it was a funerary monument of that period. Round shields carved in relief are visible on the stone blocks at the upper two corners. (Jona Lendering/Livius.org/CC0 1.0 Universal)

ABOVE RIGHT
Excavated in 1915 by a French team led by François Bonnell, the twice-burned bones of two men were found in the burial chamber. These cremated remains are believed to belong to the Numidian king Micipsa who died in 118 BC, and his son Hiempsal, who was murdered the following year. (Jona Lendering/Livius.org/CC0 1.0 Universal)

convinced of the truth of what he had heard from his [Roman] friends at Numantia, that everything at Rome was for sale' (*omnia Romae venalia esse*: *B Iug.* 20.1, cf. 8.1).

ROMANS

The Caecilii Metelli were one of the most powerful and influential families (*gentes*) in Rome at this time. Their heraldic badge was the elephant, commemorating a long-ago victory against the Carthaginians (RRC 287, 288, 292, 293, 387, 388, 390, 471). Indeed, this was the age of the Caecilii Metelli, who had held a remarkable sequence of a dozen consulships, censorships or triumphs in as many years (Vell. 2.11.3), though some, most notably Scipio Aemilianus, called them stupid (Cic. *Orat.* 2.267). Having clawed past the patrician Scipiones, who had held this position since the war with Hannibal, the Caecilii Metelli had 'prevailed by their mass and by their numbers. Their sons became consuls by prerogative or inevitable destiny; their daughters were planted out in dynastic marriages' (Syme 1956: 20).

One of the consuls of 142 BC, Lucius Caecilius Metellus Calvus, had two sons, Lucius Caecilius Metellus and **Quintus Caecilius Metellus**. The brothers too would become consuls, as would Lucius' four sons and the two sons of Quintus.

Stupid or not, Quintus Caecilius Metellus was the most respected member of this formidable political dynasty, particularly for his 'solid and unblemished reputation' (*B Iug.* 43.1) in an era when Roman politics was increasingly corrupt. He was *quaestor* in 126 BC, tribune of the plebs in 121 BC, *aedilis* in 118 BC, *praetor* in 115 BC, *propraetor* of Sicilia in 114 BC, and elected consul for 109 BC, taking command in the war against Jugurtha. In Numidia, he was not only to prove himself a disciplined and competent general but also, in contrast to his predecessors, 'displayed a disposition proof against the corrupting power of money' (*B Iug.* 43.5).

Under the Republic, Rome was ruled by pairs of annually elected magistrates, the consuls, who abdicated power at the end of the year but held absolute military and civil authority during their term of office. Lesser magistrates were also annual and in pairs, an expedient to allow them to veto each other and thereby prevent the concentration of power in one man's hands, intended to prevent the emergence of a tyrant. The principle of collegiality was basic to the Roman constitution.

A council of 300, the Senate, advised the magistrates. Theoretically, it had no constitutional powers; its decrees, which passed on a majority vote, were not law but merely consultative. As an advisory council, it discussed a whole gamut of political and religious business, but came to be particularly important in foreign affairs.

The Romans did not maintain a strict division between army and politics, and senators followed a career that brought them both military and civilian responsibilities, sometimes simultaneously. Command was thus assigned to Rome's senior magistrates, the consuls and praetors, each receiving for the duration of his office *imperium*. This was the almost mystical authority to command armies and to dispense justice, and as holders of *imperium*, they could compel absolute obedience except from someone with greater authority, *imperium maius*. What was intrinsically the power of life and death was symbolized by an axe (*secures*) enclosed in a bundle of scourging rods (*fasces*), carried by lictors, their bodyguard attendants, 12 assigned to each consul and six to each praetor.

As the chief magistrates, the two consuls provided the commanders for the most important of Rome's conflicts. Although these men owed their election primarily to their social standing rather than to any military ability, they usually led an army each: consular legions were numbered I to IIII, one consul commanding *legiones* I and III, the other *legiones* II and IIII. Unfortunately, as Roman political life forced individuals to compete rather than cooperate, the two consuls (or consul and proconsul) could often be personal or political rivals. Obviously, this did not help unity of command. Another weakness with this system was that they would all have some military experience, but often not command experience, and they were not always chosen for their generalship.

As a senatorial general received no formal training as such, he would, in fact, be expected to learn the art of generalship himself, from military

Stemma displaying the Caecilii Metelli family tree, one of the greatest noble families of the 2nd century BC. Quintus Caecilius Metellus, the most distinguished of a distinguished family, was to turn the war in Numidia around and set the stage for final victory. (Muriel Gottrop, CC BY-SA 1.0 https://creativecommons.org/licenses/by-sa/1.0, via Wikimedia Commons)

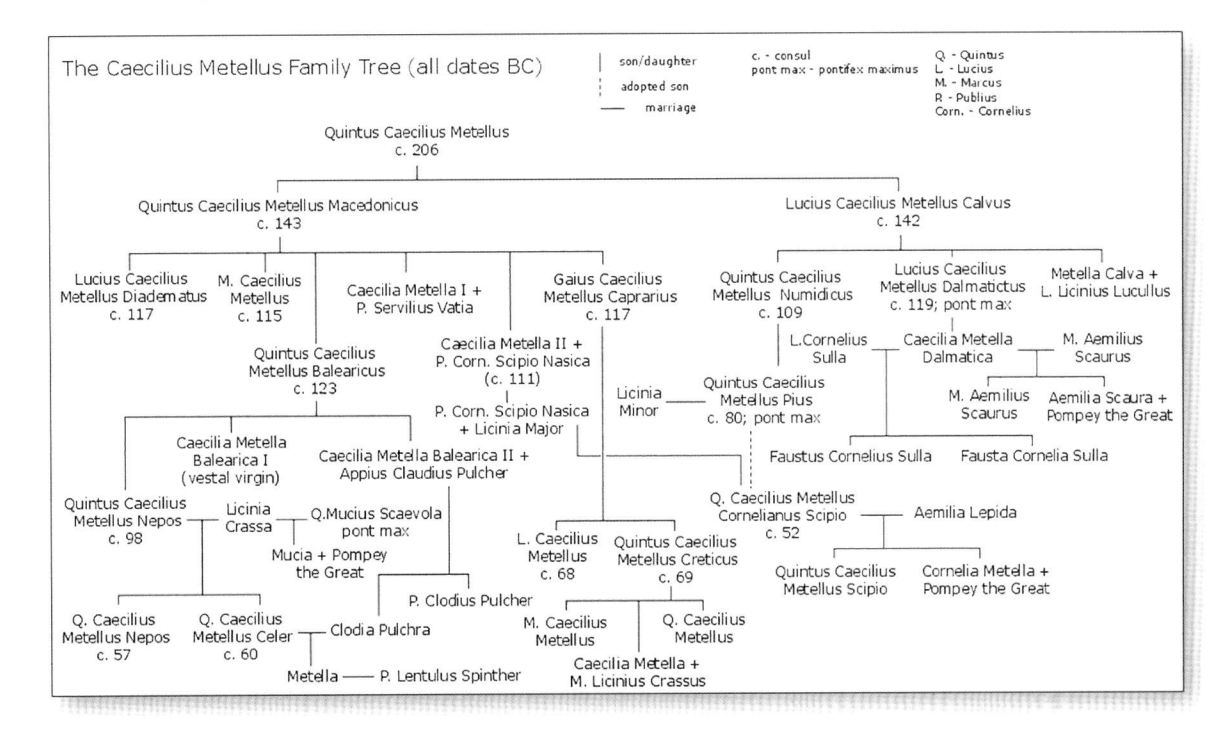

treatises (invariably Greek) or from the harder lesson of battle itself. The qualities of a good general, according to Cicero, no general himself, were 'military knowledge, courage, authority and good luck' (*De imperio Cnaeo Pompeii* 28). Still, the belief of an amateur approach to military command remained unshakable in the Roman psyche. In a speech he attributes to **Caius Marius,** who had just been elected consul, Sallust makes a telling criticism of the ineptitude of senatorial generals:

> I personally know of men, Citizens, who, after being elected consuls, have begun to study both the deeds of their forefathers and the military treatises of the Greeks; such individuals are wrongheaded, for whereas engaging in action follows upon election with respect to time, in practical experience it precedes it.
>
> Compare me now, Citizens, a *novus homo*, with those arrogant nobles. What they are accustomed to hear about or read, I have partly seen with my own eyes, in other cases done personally. What they have learned from books I have learned by service in the field. (*B Iug.* 85.12–13)

According to Marius, or so says Sallust, it is imperative to have gained experience in the field *beforehand*. No wonder the *nobilitas* were angry at this speech (Plut. *Mar.* 9).

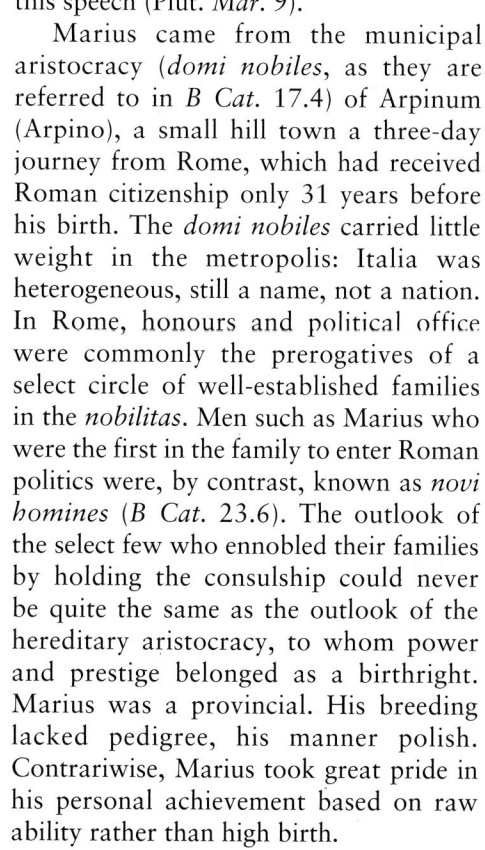

Marius came from the municipal aristocracy (*domi nobiles*, as they are referred to in *B Cat.* 17.4) of Arpinum (Arpino), a small hill town a three-day journey from Rome, which had received Roman citizenship only 31 years before his birth. The *domi nobiles* carried little weight in the metropolis: Italia was heterogeneous, still a name, not a nation. In Rome, honours and political office were commonly the prerogatives of a select circle of well-established families in the *nobilitas*. Men such as Marius who were the first in the family to enter Roman politics were, by contrast, known as *novi homines* (*B Cat.* 23.6). The outlook of the select few who ennobled their families by holding the consulship could never be quite the same as the outlook of the hereditary aristocracy, to whom power and prestige belonged as a birthright. Marius was a provincial. His breeding lacked pedigree, his manner polish. Contrariwise, Marius took great pride in his personal achievement based on raw ability rather than high birth.

Marius was born military in character, mind, intelligence and temperament: much in his later life would confirm it, and his military prowess became a regular *exemplum* in late-antique literature

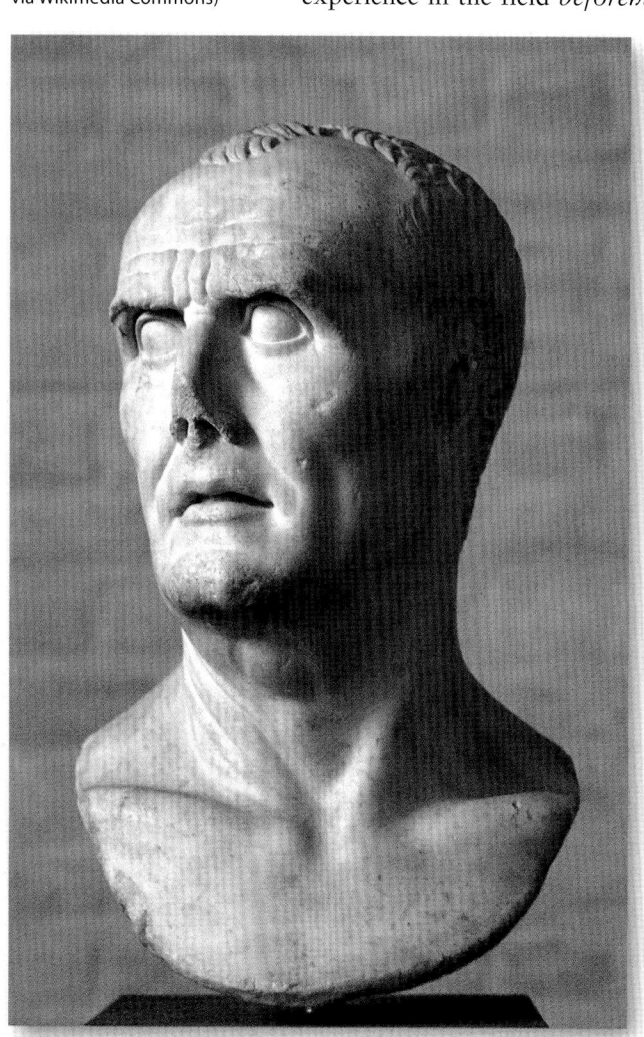

Portrait bust traditionally identified as Caius Marius (Munich, Glyptothek, inv. 319), possibly an Augustan-era marble copy of a 2nd century BC original. Marius was a controversial and pivotal figure in the Republic. Unlike Caesar or Napoleon, Marius kept no memoirs, and wrote few, if any, personal letters. He is known today chiefly through the words of enemies who not only rewrote the past in their own image, but also sought to vilify Marius and strip away his military glory. (Glyptothek, public domain, via Wikimedia Commons)

(e.g. Claudian, Eutropius). Marius began his long military career as a cavalry officer, serving with distinction under Scipio Aemilianus during the siege of Numantia. Marius (much like Jugurtha) was to enhance his reputation outside Numantia when he 'encountered and laid low an enemy in sight of his general' (Plut. *Mar.* 3.3, cf. Val. Max. 8.15.7). For a man of relatively humble origins, it must have looked as if the future belonged to him – unless his rivals devoured him first.

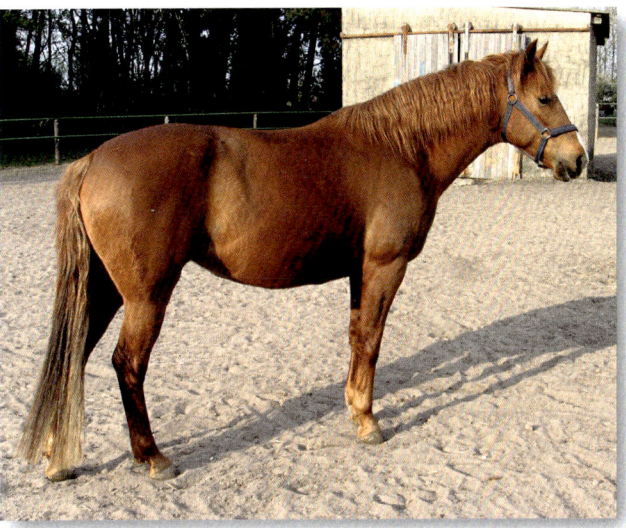

As Marius was already 23 years old at the time – six years older than the norm for commencing military service – it is feasible that he had already served on the Iberian Peninsula as early as 141 BC, when the consul Quintus Pompeius Aulus conducted a campaign against Numantia and was roundly defeated (Liv. *Per.* 54.1, App. *Iber.* 13.76–8). Plutarch hints as much when he has Marius happy to accept 'the stricter discipline which Scipio was imposing on an army that had lost much of its quality because of expensive habits and a luxurious way of life' (*Mar.* 3.2). Discipline would be another important ingredient of Marius' generalship.

One of the bonds that held Roman society together was the relationship between client (*cliens*) and patron (*patronus*). This relationship came in a wide variety of forms and guises, but all were based on the mutual exchange of favours and benefits. Roman society was thus vertically structured in terms of obligation-relationships, called clientele (*clientela*). At its crudest, a *patronus* offered protection to his *clientes*, who attended him and offered support and services in return. As the *cliens* of a privileged man might himself be the *patronus* of still less-important men, *clientelae* could be mobilized as effective voting-machines. It takes little effort, therefore, for us to appreciate how much the *patronus*–*cliens* relationship could affect the workings of the Roman state. If a *patronus* was elected to political office, his *clientela* could look forward to gaining some lucrative state contracts. The Romans saw nothing wrong or corrupt in a politician handing out state contracts to his *clientes*. It was simply how their political system worked.

Marius belonged to the *clientela* of the Caecilii Metelli. It had been in 123 BC, when Marius became *quaestor* (Val. Max. 6.9.14, cf. *Vir. ill.* 67.1), that this powerful family had taken a keen interest in his career, and so it was

ABOVE LEFT
Numidian bronze coin (Paris, Bibliothèque nationale de France, département Monnaies, inv. Vogüé 701), struck either during the reign of Masinissa or Micipsa. Reverse: rearing horse. Numidian horses, like their riders, were small and spare. Still, they were docile, hardy and well-known for their dazzling speed, and, as Livy even admits, the Numidians were 'by far the best horsemen in Africa' (29.35.8): they had a flexibility that mounted Romans and Italians could not match. (Public domain, Bibliothèque nationale de France, département Monnaies, médailles et antiques, Vogüé 701)

ABOVE RIGHT
Barb horse, a breed that originated in the coastal region of northern Africa. It is noted for its surefootedness, hardiness and stamina, with an ability to thrive on meagre rations. This horse is smaller than most breeds in stature, standing just around 140–150cm (14–15hh). It is a very fast horse. (Alexander Kastler, CC BY-SA 2.5 https://creativecommons.org/licenses/by-sa/2.5, via Wikimedia Commons)

the Caecilii Metelli who helped him to gain a plebeian tribunate in 119 BC, when he was 38 years old (Plut. *Mar.* 4.1, cf. Val. Max. 6.9.14, whose work generally emphasizes the peaks and troughs of a politician's career). Marius soon demonstrated that he was no flunky, successfully passing the *lex Maria*, a *plebiscitum* that allowed for the narrowing of the gangway across which each voter passed to fill in and deposit his ballot tablet (Cic. *Att.* 1.14.5, *Leg.* 3.17.38, RRC 292/1, cf. Plut. *Mar.* 4.2–3). To vote in the *comitia*, a man mounted one of several bridges and walked along it to a platform, where he dropped his vote in an urn. And yet, of course, the voters were in full view of everyone – in particular the senatorial aristocrats – and Marius was troubled by the likelihood of undue pressure and harassment, the Roman equivalent of voter suppression and the like.

As such, it was his patrons, the Caecilii Metelli, who blocked Marius' election to the aedileship (Plut. *Mar.* 5.1) – an office mainly concerned with public life at street level – two years later. The family intervened again when he stood for *praetor urbanus* for 115 BC, but this time they were unable to keep him out. Marius scraped in with the lowest number of votes possible, and as a consequence there were allegations of electoral bribery (*ambitus*: Val. Max. 6.9.14). In essence, bribery represented a form of patronage, a liberating force for the Roman voters, which could now market its voices. Whether this was a politically motivated prosecution or one of merit, Marius prevailed at the trial, but by the thinnest of margins. The number of votes for his guilt and innocence were dead equal, and he had to be given the benefit of the doubt (Plut. *Mar.* 5.5).

In 114 BC, Marius went to the Iberian Peninsula as *propraetor*, which was fortunate as it was a region about which he would have acquired some knowledge. As governor of Hispania Ulterior, he proved his competence, campaigning successfully against bandits while adding to his personal fortune by establishing the Iberian silver mines on a sound footing. On returning to Rome at the end of 113 BC, he married Julia (Plut. *Mar.* 6.3–4). This was a real political coup, as the Iulii Caesares were a patrician family of undoubted antiquity and prestige – though far from affluent or prominent in this age (they last held the consulship in 157 BC). Marius, for his part, not only brought his personal fortune but also his attachment to the *populares* cause in politics, something that was to prove of great benefit to his wife's nephew, Julius Caesar, in future decades.

When Marius sailed to Numidia in 109 BC as one of the *legati* under his *patronus*, Metellus, Marius had clearly set himself right with the epoch-making house of the Caecilii Metelli. It must be understood that the social gulf between the Caecilii Metelli and a man of Marius' background was great, and must have been obvious to all their contemporaries. To be sure, Metellus was to become one of the most bitter political opponents of Marius.

OPPOSING FORCES

NUMIDIANS

Horsepower
Numidian horsemen serving under Hannibal Barca had wreaked such havoc on the armies of Rome (Polyb. 3.72.10, 116.5), and under Masinissa – who, until the age of 90, could spring upon his horse's back and ride all day (Polyb. 36.16.2, 5, App. *Pun.* 16 §106, Diod. 32.16.4) – they became the prime military resource of his kingdom. By the first quarter of the 2nd century BC, Numidian horsemen were being employed, especially in Hispania, as Roman auxiliaries (e.g. Liv. 42.35.6). According to Strabo, the kings were 'much occupied with the breeding of horses thus 100,000 foals in a year have been counted with a census' (17.3.19). Numidian horses appear to have been small hardy mounts. Livy (35.11.6–11, cf. 29.34.5) describes them as small and lean in a passage that praises the Numidians' horsemanship but ridicules their appearance.

Strabo (17.3.7) singles out the small size and swiftness of African horses and, during the early Principate, the Romans particularly favoured African bloodlines for four-horse chariot racing (*CIL* VI 10047, 10053, 37834, cf. Hyland 1990: 210–14). Skeletal evidence suggests the average horse stood around 135–155cm (13.5–15.5hh) at the withers. Racing apart, such was their mastery of these small but speedy horses that the Romans made much of Numidian horsemanship, skilfully riding bareback without the use of a bridle (Liv. 21.46.5, 35.11.7, [Caes.] *B Afr.* 48.1, 62.2, Ver. 4.41, Sil. 1.215–19, Luc. 4.685).

Numidian horsemen appear as such on Trajan's Column (Scene Ixiv), though their unique hairstyle may be artistic licence and not necessarily dependent on autopsy. For although their power of endurance was often remarked upon (Polyb. 3.71.10, App. *Pun.* 2 §11, 10 §71), Numidians seem to have been frequent victims of negative stereotyping. Polybios (1.47.7, cf. *B Iug.* 54.4, 74.3, Frontin. 2.1.13) describes them as cowardly, with a tendency to flee for up to three days if beaten in battle. Livy (25.41.4, 28.44.5, 29.23.4, 30.12.18) scorns them as untrustworthy, undisciplined, hot-tempered and with more violent appetites than any other so-called

Funerary stele (Algiers, Musée national des antiquités) of a Numidian horseman, Icosium, Bab el-Oued cemetery. Originally a Phoenician colony, after the Third Punic War Icosium became part of the Roman world. Under the Principate, the Roman Army employed Numidian (and Mauretanian) horsemen in independent units. The appearance of a trooper in an *ala* was not far distant from that of a bare-backed, unbridled horse warrior of the pre-Roman past. (Jona Lendering/Livius.org/CC0 1.0 Universal)

Numidian horsemen, Trajan's Column (Scene lxiv), Rome, fighting Dacians. The Numidians are like many Roman depictions of non-Roman troops, namely very much stylized – e.g. hair in tightly curled ringlets or braided (see Strab. 17.3.7), though it must be said the artist did depict the braided bosals and their distinctive small round shields. They wear short, baggy sleeveless tunics, probably undyed wool, pinned at the shoulders and belted. The metal detail has not survived, but these horsemen, as indicated by the drill holes, originally grasped javelins in their right hands. Numidian horsemen, lightly equipped and exceedingly agile, were brilliant skirmishers, and on campaign were ideal for foraging, reconnaissance and ambush. (Benjamín Núñez González, CC BY-SA 4.0 https://creativecommons.org/licenses/by-sa/4.0, via Wikimedia Commons)

barbarians. Aelianus maligns the Numidians as 'slim and dirty like the horses they ride', and while praising their ability to endure fatigue, denigrates the care that they gave their horses, saying 'they neither rub them down, roll them, clean their hooves, comb manes, plait forelocks, nor wash them when tired, but when dismounted turn them loose to graze' (3.2).

Worth noting, though, lazy or not, turning a horse loose to graze immediately after a tough ride is the best treatment it can have and often prevents muscle and limb ailments. As Appianus points out, the Numidian lifestyle and horse management was geared for their rugged way of life: 'The Numidians also know how to endure hunger. They often subsist on herbs in place of bread, and they drink nothing but water. Their horses never even taste grain; they feed on grass alone and drink but rarely' (App. *Pun.* 2 §11). Numidians may have ridden small, swift horses that appeared scrawny, but they were capable of enduring in harsh terrain where heavier, stall-fed mounts could not.

Clearly one with his mount, riding bareback rather than firmly seated on the four-horned rigid saddle employed by Celtic and Roman horsemen at the time, the Numidian horseman expertly guided his horse with just a bosal. This was a rope or noseband 'made of cotton or of hair, from which hangs a leading-rein' (Strab. 17.3.7). Without the use of bridle or a metal bit in the horse's mouth, or even the prick spurs commonly used by Greek and Roman riders for that matter, Numidians were obviously not heavy-handed riders; the majority of their direction in riding came from their legs. Livy (23.29.5) records that some Numidians would even engage the enemy accompanied by a spare horse, onto which they would jump when their first mount began to tire, even in the thick of battle.

In battle, Numidian horsemen relied upon two or three javelins. Particularly effective when thrown from horseback, a javelin differed from the spear in that it was lighter, so permitting a man to attack from a decent distance. Swords are absent from nearly all iconography depicting Numidian horsemen: they do not appear in the Abizar series of stelae. Livy reinforces this when he twice notes their lack of secondary weaponry: in action against the Ligures in 193 BC (35.11.7), and in an act of subterfuge at Cannae in 216 BC, when a unit of 500 Numidian horsemen concealed swords beneath their tunics, he comments these were not their customary weapons (22.48.1). For personal protection, horsemen carried shields.

Strabo (17.3.7) notes that African tribes made their shields of rawhide, predominantly elephant hide. This is very thick – up to 2.5cm on the back of the animal – and when dried in the sun produces very taut and tough leather, perfect for making the faces of shields. The frame of the shield was probably of wicker, which could have been woven into a circle rigid enough to hold the thick sheets of elephant hide in the correct shape, while remaining quite stiff and resistant, but very light. Sallust says that when a picked band of Roman soldiers had to scale a rock face to enter one of Jugurtha's fortresses, rather than their own heavy *scuta* they chose to carry Numidian shields made of hide 'because of their lighter weight' (*B Iug.* 94.1).

Armed with a handful of javelins and protected by a lightweight shield, the Numidian horseman was the master of hit-and-run warfare, depending on baffling their opponents by their almost hallucinatory speed and bird-like agility (Polyb. 3.116.5, App. *Pun.* 2 §11, Caes. *B civ.* 2.41, [Caes.] *B Afr.* 14–15, 70.2, 71.2, Frontin. 1.5.16).

Gathering of the tribes

In war, Numidian tribal troops followed their own chieftains, armed service being due to the tribal leader, who in turn owed it to the king. Such forces could be raised quickly, but also melted away at sowing or harvesting time. Obviously, observance of the agriculture cycle was an inherent weakness in tribal armies, and as Sallust puts it, these hastily raised levies were 'lacklustre and weak, being more accustomed to tending fields and flocks than war' (*B Iug.* 54.3).

At the outset of the Jugurthine War, these tribal forces were prepared to face the Romans in open battle, but after battle at the Muthul, Jugurtha switched to the more advantageous art of ambushing the enemy in terrain of his own choosing. So, much like their cavalry counterparts, the Numidian infantry would now rely on mobility as their defence, and engaged their enemy from a distance.

A contemporary bosal fitted to a horse. The word bosal (or bozal) is from the Spanish, literally 'muzzle', and was used in the hackamore of the vaquero tradition. Of braided rawhide and fitted to a horse in a manner that allows it to rest quietly until the rider uses the reins to give a signal. It acts upon the horse's nose and jaw. Support is provided by a headstall, an item of horse tack that does not appear on representations of a Numidian bosal. This was a simple braided rope or rawhide band about the horse's neck by which the rider could exert a little control. Strabo (17.3.7) mentions that the rider could also control his horse by a stick, probably by tapping with it between the ears. (Montanabw, CC BY-SA 3.0 https://creativecommons.org/licenses/by-sa/3.0, via Wikimedia Commons)

Stèle d'Abizar (Algiers, Musée national des antiquités), one of a series of pre-Roman stelae from Abizar, Algeria, depicting a bearded Numidian horseman (*Encyclopédie Berbère* 1: *s.v.* Abizar), dated to the time Jugurtha waged an insurgent war against Rome. He is armed with three javelins and carries a small, round shield. The incised circle in the centre suggests the shield was bossed. The best tribal warriors were horsemen – especially those from the arid steppe areas of the Sahara where the nomadic life still prevailed – though the bulk of Numidian armies were composed of lightly armed foot warriors. (Meriam Cherif, CC BY-SA 4.0 https://creativecommons.org/licenses/by-sa/4.0, via Wikimedia Commons)

The hardscrabble living that made them tough also meant that the tribal warriors were poorly equipped. Broad-bladed javelins rather than bows were the commonest missile weapons of all peoples along the northern African littoral. Javelins could be equipped with a finger loop, a thin leather thong that provided leverage and acted like a sling to propel the missile, and as it was launched the thong unwound, having the same effect as the rifling inside a rifle barrel: it spun the javelin, ensuring a steadier flight. Another personal weapon was the arm dagger, which was housed in a leather sheath attached to the inner side of his left forearm by a leather loop. For quick extraction with the right hand, the flat wooden hilt rested against the inside of the warrior's left wrist. Like their mounted brethren, tribal warriors carried small round, hide shields.

The best warriors may have been horsemen – especially those from the arid steppe areas of the Sahara where the nomadic life still prevailed – but the bulk of Numidian armies were composed of lightly armed tribal warriors. Yet the most powerful kings of Numidia, such as Jugurtha, also raised an elite force of slaves, freedmen and mercenaries paid through taxation. Such formations were probably based upon the Roman model and even seem to have abided Roman training and discipline (*B Iug.* 80.2). Well trained and better equipped, these men also carried swords, mostly stripped from Roman prisoners or corpses. For Jugurtha, such units formed a praetorian guard of sorts, to protect his position and so prevent his adoptive brothers' fate befalling him. Little is known of their origins, though they did include Thracians and Ligurum deserters (*B Iug.* 38.6, App. *Num.* fr. 3, cf. *B Iug.* 56.2, 62.6).

Jugurtha had shown streaks of opportunism to penetrate or influence the Roman army in Numidia. Specifically, Sallust talks of Jugurtha's nefarious use of agents during the Roman operations around Suthul (location unknown) in late 110 BC, '[T]hrough cunning men he worked upon the Roman army day and night, bribing the *centuriones* and commanders of cavalry *turmae* either to desert or to abandon their posts at a given signal' (*B Iug.* 38.3). The *turmae* in question were drawn chiefly from Rome's allies, and those that did desert on this occasion were Thracians, while it was the chief centurion (*centurio primi pili*) of *legio* III who 'gave the enemy a place of entry through the fortification [of the marching camp] he had been appointed to guard' (*B Iug.* 38.6).

Jugurtha's contingent at Numantia included 'twelve elephants and the body of archers and slingers who usually accompanied them in war' (App. *Iber.* 14 §89, cf. Frontin. 4.7.27). Presumably these men were tasked both to inflict casualties upon the enemy in combined action with the elephants and defend them from attacks by the enemy.

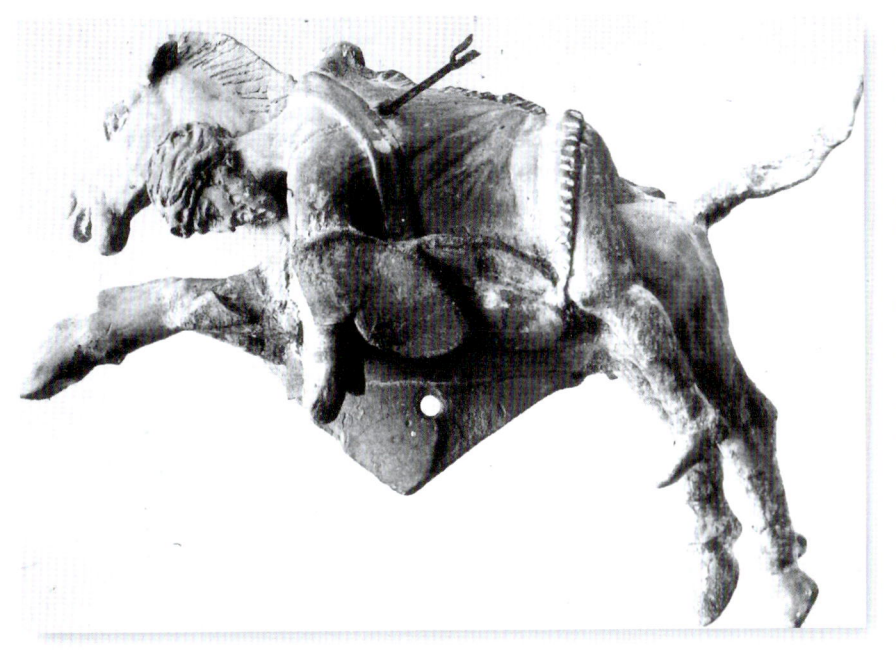

Appliqué terracotta attachment (Paris, Musée du Louvre, inv. Cp 5223) from a tomb in Canusium (Canosa di Puglia, Italy), late 3rd–early 2nd century BC, in the form of a wounded Numidian horseman. He wears a short, woollen fringed tunic and carries a small round shield. A sword is suspended from a baldric on his left side, which is an atypical weapon for Numidians and suggests this is a portrayal of a tribal chieftain. This figurine was probably part of the decoration belonging to a funnel jar. (© Nic Fields)

Like Syphax and Masinissa before him, Jugurtha would combine the military skills learned while fighting with the Romans with the classic Numidian use of cavalry, which were the finest of irregular horse, and wily guerrilla tactics (e.g. *B Iug.* 50.4–6, 54.9–10, 55.8). The king was clearly at home practising what we call asymmetric warfare – considered an unfair confrontation to conventional, infantry-based armies.

ROMANS

By the time Rome was no longer the hilltop palisaded village nestling on the left bank of the Tiber, Roman warfare had become an adaptation of

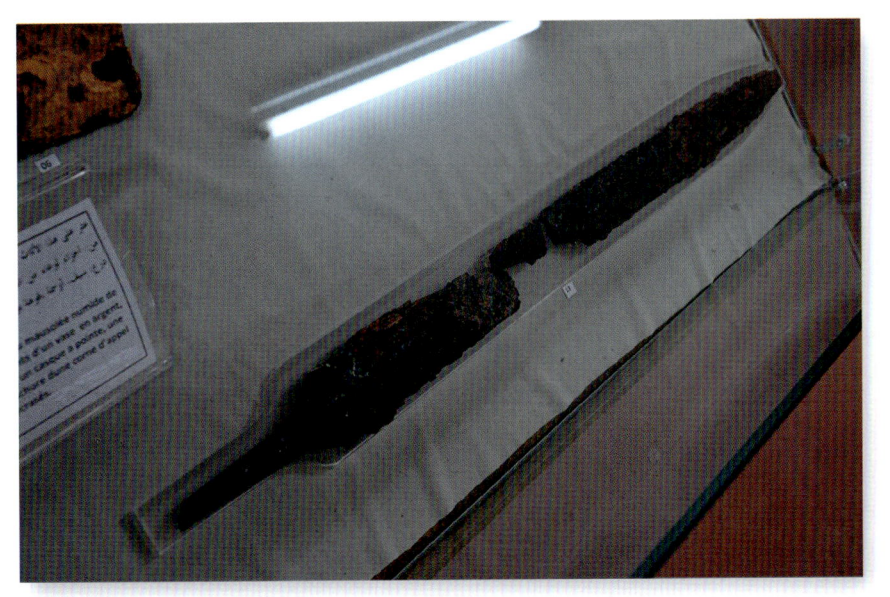

Iron sword (Constantine, Musée national Cirta) from the Mausoleum Soumaā d'el-Khroub, *c.* 120 BC. The surviving blade is 67cm long and 5cm wide with edges that were parallel for most of their length before tapering to a sharp point 15cm from the tip. The hilt and pommel have long disappeared but the high phosphorous content of the metal tang shows that the grip was made of a material of bone, horn or ivory, and not of wood. According to Feugère (1993: 79–81), the sword was originally 70.5cm long and should perhaps be included among the group of known Roman Republican *gladii*. The hilt had been decorated with gold and copper and was housed in a scabbard of sandalwood and riveted leather. Unless given as a gift, it was possibly acquired in battle. (Jona Lendering/Livius.org/CC0 1.0 Universal)

Iron mail shirt (Constantine, Musée national Cirta) from the Mausoleum Soumaā d'el-Khroub, *c.* 120 BC and possibly Roman in origin (gift or booty). Ring mail was expensive to produce, so its use would have been mainly restricted to those who could afford it. It was manufactured from alternating rows of solid rings and rows of riveted rings; each being linked through its four neighbours. The solid rings were made by punching holes in iron sheets. The riveted rings were formed from iron wires with their ends butted together. The rivet to secure the flattened ends of riveted rings was a small triangular chip of metal, closed with a pair of tongs with recessed jaws. There were 35,000 to 40,000 rings in the completed armour. (Jona Lendering/Livius.org/CC0 1.0 Universal)

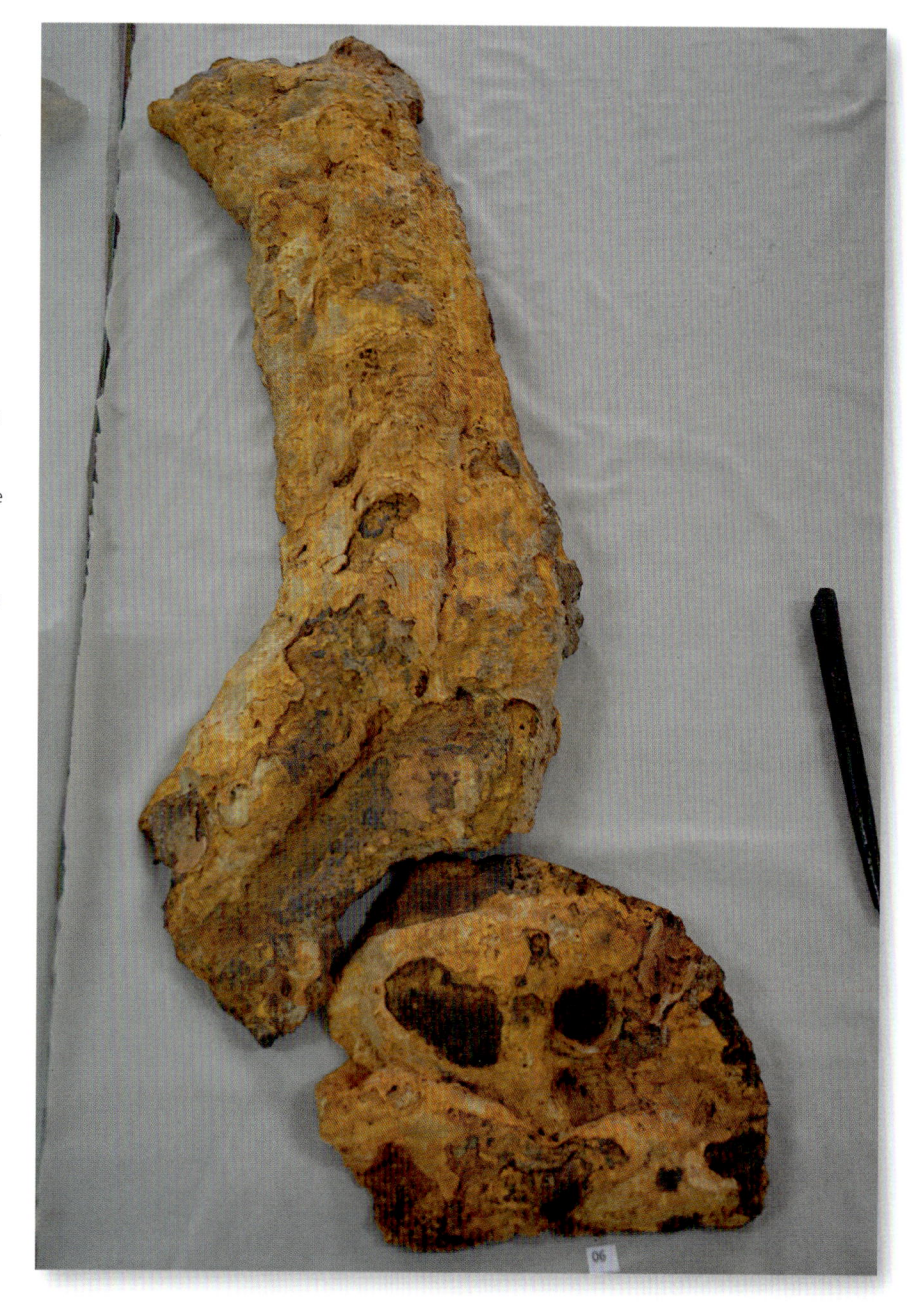

Greek warfare and the hoplite ideology of the decisive battle. Yet when Rome was no longer the humble city of the seven hills, the army had assumed the more familiar form of the manipular legion. In both these instances, the model is that of the disciplined infantry formation in a set-piece battle, first with the rigid phalanx and then with the more flexible legion, but both with an excellence in and a preference for a head-to-head encounter that seeks to destroy the enemy. In this decisive clash of opposing armies, the Roman legion usually performed very well, returning any blows vigorously and viciously. The Roman citizen soldier, like his Greek counterpart, excelled at close quarter combat, but his legion could be manoeuvred more readily than the phalanx. In contrast to the one solid block of the Greeks, the legion was now divided into several small blocks, with spaces between them. The Romans, in other words, gave the phalanx 'joints' in order to increase efficiency and flexibility.[3] Additionally, each soldier now had twice as much elbow room for individual action, which involved swordplay.

We have two accounts of the manipular legion's organization. First, the Roman historian Livy, writing more than three centuries after the event, describes the legion of the mid-4th century BC. Second, the Greek historian Polybios, a captive living and writing in Rome at the time (a rare example of history not being written by victors), describes the legion of the mid-2nd century BC. The transition between the Livian and Polybian legion is somewhat obscure, but for the sake of brevity and clarity, we need only concern ourselves with the Polybian legion.

Polybios breaks off his narrative of the Second Punic War at the nadir of Rome's fortunes, following the triple defeats of the Trebbia, Lake Trasimene and Cannae, and turns to an extended digression on the constitution and the army of Rome (Polyb. 6.11–18 [constitution], 19–42 [army]). Polybios clearly admired Rome's political setup and military system. Still, there is no obvious liking of Roman power, just a clear-eyed explanation of how the Romans achieved it: Polybios was no card-carrying, pro-Roman Greek.

ABOVE LEFT
Stele (Constantine, Musée national Cirta, inv. 3C), El Hofra sanctuary near Cirta, 2nd century BC. The images on the stele represent a spearhead and a *thyreós*, a flat, oval shield with a metal strip boss reinforcing a wooden spindle boss. (Reda Kerbush, CC BY-SA 4.0 https://creativecommons.org/licenses/by-sa/4.0, via Wikimedia Commons)

ABOVE RIGHT
Funerary stele (Istanbul, Arkeoloji Müzesi, inv. 1141F) of Salmamodes of Adada, 300–50 BC. A Seleukid *thōrakítēs*, he wears an iron mail shirt lacking shoulder pieces and carries a *thyreós*. The *thōrakítai* were armoured but mobile infantry (Polyb. 10.29.6). A *thyreós* and an iron mail shirt were found in the Mausoleum Soumaā d'el-Khroub. (DeFly94, CC BY-SA 4.0 https://creativecommons.org/licenses/by-sa/4.0, via Wikimedia Commons)

---

3 It was the doyen of modern military historians, Hans Delbrück (1975: 275), who first characterized the Roman legion as a phalanx with joints.

Punic silver double shekel (Berlin, Münzkabinett der Staatlichen Museen, inv. 18204013), 237–209 BC. Obverse: garlanded bust of Melqart/Herakles. Reverse: Punic war elephant with driver wearing a long-hooded cloak. Because of its small stature, the African forest elephant did not carry the turret but only its driver (see Scullard 1974: 240–5). The driver, who was perhaps brought especially from India in the early days, managed his charge, sitting astride its neck, armed only with a hooked elephant goad, *ankus*, as seen on this coin. Eventually, they were provided with a mallet and sharp chisel with which to pole-axe their beasts, by a swift blow to the base of the skull, if they went into reverse and ran amok. The primary purpose of Numidian war elephants was to frighten the enemy, particularly open-order infantry or horsemen whose mounts were unaccustomed to the sight and smell of them. (Reinhard Saczewski, Münzkabinett, Staatliche Museen zu Berlin - Stiftung Preußischer Kulturbesitz, 18204013)

Polybian legion

The Roman Army was based on the principle of personal service by the citizens defending their state. It was not yet a professional army. The term *legio* (levy) obviously referred to the entire citizen force raised by Rome in any one year, but by at least the 4th century BC, it had come to denote the most significant subdivision of the army. Then, as Rome's territory and population increased, it was found necessary to levy two consular armies, each of two *legiones* (legions). Accompanying each legion were soldiers provided by Rome's Latin and Italian allies, the *socii* (Polyb. 6.26.7). Their principal unit was known as the *ala* (wing), which deployed the same number and type of infantry as their Roman counterparts. By the time of Hannibal, if not before, in a standard consular army, the two Roman *legiones* would form the centre with two Latin/Italian *alae* deployed on their flanks – they were known as *ala sinistra* (left wing), and *ala dextra* (right wing) (ibid. 26.9). According to Livy (9.30.3), the latest possible date for the regular number of legions to double to four was 311 BC. Polybios (3.109.12) has Rome levying and supporting four active legions each year for annual service with the two consuls, which were supplemented by an equal number of soldiers provided by the *socii*.

All citizens between 17 and 46 years of age who satisfied the property criteria, namely those who owned property above the value of 11,000 *asses*, were required by the Senate to attend a selection process, the *dilectus*, on the Capitol. Citizens were liable for 16 years' service as a legionary (*miles*) or ten as a horseman (*eques*) (Polyb. 6.19.2). These figures represent the maximum that a man could be called upon to serve. In the 2nd century BC, for instance, a man was normally expected to serve up to six years in a continuous posting, after which he expected to be released from his military oath. Thereafter he was liable for enlistment, as an *evocatus*, up to the maximum of 16 campaigns or years. Some men might serve for a single year at a time, and be obliged to come forward again at the next *dilectus*, until their full six-year period was completed.

At the *dilectus*, the citizens were arranged into some semblance of soldierly order by height and age. They were then brought forward four at a time to be selected for service in one of the four consular legions being raised that year. The junior military tribunes of each legion took it in turns to have first choice, thus ensuring an even distribution of experience and quality

Leaf-shaped spearheads (x2), short but broad-bladed javelin heads (x2), and pointed butt-spikes (x4), all of iron (Constantine, Musée national Cirta), from the Mausoleum Soumaâ d'el-Khroub, *c*.120 BC. Spears and javelins are difficult to classify, for many spears could be used for either thrusting or for throwing. As for the Numidians, unlike their Roman opponents, both foot and horse were lightly armed, with the javelin being favoured as a range weapon. Those javelin heads found in the mausoleum vary in length but are mostly around 30cm long and 4cm at their widest point, with a circular socket 1.2cm in diameter at the base for the attachment of a slender wooden shaft. For side arms, Numidians carried daggers – and perhaps the occasional sword – often supplied by or taken from the Romans, though close-quarter work was by and large shunned. (Jona Lendering/Livius.org/CC0 1.0 Universal)

throughout the four units. They then ordered the soldiers to take a formal oath. Though the exact text of the oath is not given by Polybios, he does say a soldier swore 'he would obey his officers and carry out their commands to the best of his ability' (6.21.1). To speed up the process, the oath was sworn in full by one man, and each of the rest swore that he would do the same as the first, perhaps using the phrase '*idem in me*' ('the same for me'). They were given a date and muster point, and then dismissed to their homes.

The standard complement of the Polybian legion was 4,200 foot and 300 horse, in theory if not practice (Polyb. 6.20.8–9),[4] and consisted of five elements – the close-order infantry, *hastati*, *principes*, and *triarii*, the open-order infantry, *velites*, and the cavalry, *equites* – each equipped differently and having specific places in the legion's tactical formation. Its principal strength was the 30 maniples of its close-order infantry, the *velites* and *equites* acting in support of these. Its organization allowed it only one standard formation, the *triplex acies* with three successive, relatively shallow lines of ten maniples each, these fighting units supporting each other to apply maximum pressure on an enemy to the front.

Hence, the legion was divided horizontally into three lines, and vertically into maniples, *manipuli*, with the first line containing 1,200 *hastati* in ten maniples of 120, the second line 1,200 *principes* organized in the same way, and the third line of 600 *triarii* also in ten maniples. The *hastati* (spearmen) were men in the flower of youth, the *principes* (chief men) in the prime of manhood, and the *triarii* (third-rank men) the oldest and more mature men (Polyb. 6.21.7).[5] Of the 4,200 legionaries in a legion, 3,000 served as close-order infantry, and the remaining 1,200 men, the youngest and poorest, served as lightly armed infantry. Known as *velites* (cloak-wearers), they were divided for administrative purpose among the legionaries of the maniples, each maniple being allocated the same number of *velites* (ibid. 21.7, 24.4). Finally, accompanying the legionaries were 300 fellow citizens on horseback, the *equites*.

---

4 Elsewhere Polybios refers to the standard complement of 4,000 infantry and 300 cavalry (1.16.2) and of 4,000 infantry and 200 cavalry (3.107.10), and does suggest that there were sometimes fewer than 4,000 infantry per legion (6.21.10).

5 The same order for the three lines appears elsewhere in Polybios' narrative (14.8.5, 15.9.7), and in Livy's also (30.8.5, 32.11, 34.10), as well as in other antiquarian sources (e.g. Varro *de lingua Latina* 5.89).

Caliga (London, British Museum), from Qasr Ibrim, Egypt, 1st century BC. The heavy-soled hobnailed footwear worn by legionaries consisted of a fretwork upper, a thin insole and a thicker outer sole made of several layers of cow or ox leather glued together and studded with hobnails. The one-piece upper was sewn up at the heel and laced up the centre of the foot to the top of the ankle with a leather thong. The open design, which allowed for free passage of air and, more importantly, water, was specifically designed so as to reduce the likelihood of blisters, as well as other incapacitating foot conditions such as trench foot, a severe fungal infection caused by wearing wet boots over a long period. (Prioryman, CC BY-SA 4.0 https://creativecommons.org/licenses/by-sa/4.0, via Wikimedia Commons)

Polybian legionary

The Romans attached a great deal of importance to training, and it is this that largely explains the formidable success of their army. 'And what can I say about the training of legions?' is the rhetorical question aired by Cicero. 'Put an equally brave, but untrained soldier in the front line and he will look like a woman' (*Tusc.* 2.16.37). The basic aim of this training was to give the legions superiority over the 'barbarian' in battle, and in the 4th century AD, Vegetius would attribute 'the conquest of the world by the Roman people' to their training methods, camp discipline and military skills (1.1).

The Romans took great pride in their ability to learn from their enemies too, copying weaponry (and tactics) from successive opponents and often improving upon them. This was one of their strong points and, as Polybios rightly says, 'no people are more willing to adopt new customs and to emulate what they see is better done by others' (6.25.10).

The *hastati* and *principes* carried the Italic oval, semi-cylindrical body shield, conventionally known as the *scutum*, the Iberian cut-and-thrust sword, *gladius Hispaniensis*, and two sorts of javelin, *pilum*, heavy and light. The *triarii* were similarly equipped, except they carried a long thrusting spear, *hasta*, instead of the *pilum* (Polyb. 6.23.6). This 2m weapon survived from the era when the Roman Army was a hoplite militia: Dionysios of Halikarnassos says 'cavalry spears' (i.e. hoplite spears: 20.11.2) were still being employed in battle by the *principes* during the war with Pyrrhos (280–275 BC). Apart from those carried by the *triarii*, the *hasta* was obsolete in Polybios' day. The close-quarter, battering power of the legion was thus provided by the legionary wielding *pilum* and *gladius*, and the combination of *pilum* shower and blade work rendered the Roman Army so deadly.

In the Livian legion there is no reference to the *pilum*, which, if Livy's account is accepted, may not yet have been introduced. The earliest reference to the *pilum* belongs to 293 BC during the Third Samnite War (Liv. 10.39.12, cf. Plut. *Pyrr.* 21.9); though the earliest authentic use of this weapon may belong to 251 BC (Polyb. 1.40.12). The *pilum*, therefore, was probably adopted from Iberian mercenaries fighting for Carthage during the First Punic War.

Polybios distinguishes two types of *pilum*, 'thick' and 'thin', saying each man had both types (6.23.9–11). Surviving examples from the site of the Roman siege of Numantia (134–133 BC) confirm two basic types of construction. Both have a small pyramid-shaped point at the end of a narrow soft-iron shank, fitted to a wooden shaft some 1.4m in length. One type has the shank socketed, while the other has a wide flat iron tang riveted to a thickened section of the wooden shaft. The last type is probably Polybios' 'thick' *pilum*, referring to the broad joint of iron and wood. This broad section can be either square or round in section, and is strengthened by a small iron ferrule. The iron shank varies in length, with many examples averaging around 70cm. The 'thin' *pilum* is described merely as a weapon similar to a hunting javelin of average dimensions.

All of the weapon's weight was concentrated behind the small pyramidal tip, giving it great penetrative power. The length of the iron shank gave it the reach to punch through an enemy's shield and still go on to wound his body, but even if it failed to do so and merely stuck in the shield it was very difficult to pull free and might force the man to discard his weighed-down shield and fight unprotected. A useful side effect of this 'armour piercing' weapon was that the narrow shank would often bend on impact, ensuring that the enemy would not throw it back. The maximum range of the *pilum* was some 30m, but its effective range something like half that. Throwing a *pilum* at close range would have improved both accuracy and armour penetration.

A later lexicographer, possibly following Polybios' lost account of the Iberian War, says the *gladius Hispaniensis* was adopted from the Iberians (or Celtiberians) at the time of the war with Hannibal, but it is possible that this weapon, along with the *pilum*, was adopted from Iberian mercenaries serving Carthage during the First Punic

Celtiberian antenna-hilted iron sword and biglobular-hilted iron dagger (Soria, Museo Numantino de Soria) from Montejo de Tiermes, 3rd–2nd century BC. These Celtiberian weapons were the precursors of the *gladius Hispaniensis* and the *pugio* carried by legionaries. Note the ring suspension system attached to the scabbard of the dagger, likewise taken up by the Romans. (Jl FilpoC, CC BY-SA 4.0 https://creativecommons.org/licenses/by-sa/4.0, via Wikimedia Commons)

War (Polyb. fr. 179 with Walbank 1957: 704). It was certainly in use by 197 BC, when Livy (31.34.4) describes the Macedonians' shock at the terrible wounds it inflicted. The Iberians used a relatively short, but deadly sword. This was either the *falcata*, an elegant, curved single-bladed weapon derived from the Greek *kópis*, most common in the south and south-east of the Iberian Peninsula, or the cut-and-thrust sword, straight-bladed weapon from which the *gladius* was derived (Polyb. 3.114.2–4, Liv. 22.46.6).

The earliest Roman specimens date to 3rd–1st century BC, but a 4th-century BC sword of similar shape has been found in Spain at the cemetery of Los Cogotes (Avila), as is an earlier Iberian example from Atienza. The Roman blade could be as much as 64–69cm in length and 4.8–6cm wide and waisted in the centre. It was a fine piece of 'blister steel' with a triangular point between 9.6cm and 20cm long and honed down razor-sharp edges, and was designed to puncture armour. It had a comfortable bone handgrip grooved to fit the fingers, and a large spherical pommel, usually of wood or ivory, to help with counterbalance. Extant examples weigh between 1.2kg and 1.6kg. The story of the *gladius* is an object lesson of the Roman way of taking the best of what others have learned and making it their own.

The legionary also carried a dagger, *pugio*. The dagger was the ultimate weapon of last resort. However, it was probably more often employed in the commonplace tasks of living on campaign. Like the *gladius*, the Roman dagger was borrowed from the Iberians and then developed.

Polybios (6.23.14–15) says all soldiers wore a bronze pectoral, a span (223mm) square, to protect the heart and chest, although those who could afford it would wear instead an iron mail shirt, *lorica hamata*. He also adds that a bronze helmet was worn, without describing it, but the Montefortino and Etrusco-Corinthian styles were popular at this time and were probably all used, as they certainly all were by later Roman troops. He does say helmets were crested with a circlet of feathers and three upright black or crimson feathers a cubit (444mm) tall (Polyb. 6.23.12–13), so exaggerating the wearer's height. Interestingly, Polybios (6.23.8) clearly refers to only one greave being worn, and Arrianus (*Ars Tactica* 3.5), writing more or less three centuries later, confirms this, saying the ancient Romans used to wear one greave only, on the leading leg, the left. Undoubtedly many of those who could afford it would actually choose to wear a pair of bronze greaves, so covering each leg from ankle to knee.

To complete his defensive equipment, each soldier carried the *scutum*, an Italic body shield probably derived from the Samnites (Walbank 1957: 703–4, Cornell 1995: 170). Polybios (6.23.2–5) describes the *scutum* in detail, and his

Full-scale reconstruction of Roman *lorica hamata* (Alise-Sainte-Reine, MuséoParc Alésia). Combining strength with flexibility and airiness, mail consisted of a matrix of alternatively riveted and solid iron rings, each being linked through its four neighbours. Very laborious to make, the problem was partly overcome by the introduction of alternate rows of solid rings, which did not require being riveted. Mail armour was an effective protection against bladed weapons, but in comparison to scale and lamellar armour it was less effective as a protection against arrows and blunt weapons. (© Esther Carré)

account is confirmed by the remarkable discovery in 1900 of a shield of this type at Kasr-el-Harit in the Fayûm, Egypt (Connolly 1998: 132). It is midway between a rectangle and an oval in shape, and is 1.28m in length and 63.5cm in width with a slight concavity. It is constructed from three layers of birch laths, each layer laid at right angles to the next, and originally covered with lamb's wool felt. This was likely fitted damp in one piece, which, when dry, had shrunk and strengthened the whole artefact. The shield board is thicker in the centre and flexible at the edges, making it very resilient to blows, and the top and bottom edges may have been reinforced with bronze or iron edging to prevent splitting. Nailed to the front and running vertically from top to bottom is a wooden spine, *spina*. Good protection came at a price, for the *scutum* was heavy, weights of reconstructions range from 5.5kg to 10kg (Republican models being heavier than that of the Principate), and in battle its entire weight was borne by the left arm as the soldier held the horizontal handgrip behind the bronze or iron boss, *umbo*, which reinforced the *spina*.

Finally, these short-term citizen soldiers provided their own equipment and therefore we should expect considerably more variation in clothing, armour and weapons than the legionaries of the later professional legions. There is no good reason to believe, for instance, that they wore tunics of the same hue or that shields were adorned with unit insignia. In fact, Polybios makes no mention of shield decoration, despite his detailed description of legionary equipment down to the colour of their plumes. This seems to be supported by sculptural evidence, such as the Aemilius Paullus monument or the Altar of Domitius Ahenobarbus, which show *scuta* left plain.

Lightly armed infantry

The *velites* were armed with the *gladius Hispaniensis* according to Livy (38.21.15), and a bundle of javelins, each with a wooden shaft only two cubits (93cm) long, and a finger thick, topped with a long thin iron head a span (23cm) in length, which bent at the first impact (Polyb. 6.22.4). For protection, they wore a helmet without a crest and carried a round shield but wore no armour. In order to be distinguished from a distance, some *velites* would cover their unadorned helmets with a wolf's skin or something similar (ibid. 22.1–3).

ABOVE LEFT
Etrusco-Corinthian helmet type B (Museo civico archeologico di Milano) of bronze, 450–400 BC. Another Italic pattern commonly worn by legionaries, it was particularly associated with the *triarii* and senior officers. This example is missing its Attic-type cheek pieces and the characteristic three-pronged crest holder. Italic development of the classic Corinthian helmet much used by Greek hoplites, the Etrusco-Corinthian pattern was designed to be worn as a cap. (© José Luiz Bernardes Ribeiro, CC-BY-SA-3.0 https://creativecommons.org/licenses/by-sa/3.0, via Wikimedia Commons)

ABOVE RIGHT
Detail on 3rd-century BC alabaster cinerary urn (Palermo, Museo Archeologico di Palermo, inv. 8461) depicting two Etruscan warriors wearing crested Etrusco-Corinthian helmets. (© Nic Fields)

ABOVE
Panel I of the frieze from the Monument of Aemilius Paullus (Delphi, Museum of Archaeology) erected at the sanctuary of Apollo, Delphi, to commemorate his victory over Perseus of Macedon at Pydna (22 June 168 BC). To the right, a legionary bears a *scutum*. Using an overhand grip, he is holding it by a single horizontal handgrip. This enables him to comfortably carry his shield with the arm at full stretch. The *scutum* was used both defensively and offensively. To be light enough to be held continually in battle, the *scutum* was constructed of double or triple thickness plywood, covered with canvas and calfskin. To prevent splitting, iron binding protected its top and bottom. (Colin Whiting, CC BY-SA 4.0 https://creativecommons.org/licenses/by-sa/4.0, via Wikimedia Commons)

BELOW
Detail from the Altar of Domitius Ahenobarbus (Paris, Musée du Louvre, inv. Ma 975), depicting two chatting legionaries while an *eques* steadies the horse. Clearly depicted are *scuta*, each with a sheet metal (copper alloy or iron) *umbo*, which is reinforcing the *spina*. (© Esther Carré)

As for the number of javelins carried, Polybios does not specify. Livy (26.4.4), on the other hand, says *velites* had seven such javelins, *iacula*, while the 2nd-century BC Roman satirist Lucilius (*Satires* 7.290) has them carrying five each. Even so, in firepower they were no match for slingers and archers, either in range or quantity of ammunition. But they could move fast.

Cavalry

Each legion had a small cavalry force of 300, organized in ten *turmae* of 30 horsemen each (Polyb. 6.20.8–9, 25.1, cf. 2.24.13, Liv. 3.62). The military tribunes appointed three *decuriones* to each *turma*, of whom the senior commanded with the rank of *praefectus*. Each *decurio* (leader of ten) chose an *optio* as his second-in-command and rear-rank officer (Polyb. 6.25.1–2). This organization suggests that the *turma* was divided into three files of ten.

These files were obviously not independent tactical subunits, for the *turma* was evidently intended to operate as a single entity, as indicated by the seniority of one *decurio* over his two colleagues.

The *equites* formed the most prestigious element of the legion, and were recruited from the wealthiest citizens able to afford a horse and its trappings (Polyb. 6.20.9). By our period, these included the top 18 centuries (*centuriae*) of the voting assembly, the *comitia centuriata*, who were rated *equites equo publico*, the equestrian elite, obliging the state to provide them with the cost of a remount should their horse be killed on active service. The elder Cato was later to boast that his grandfather had five horses killed under him in battle and replaced by the state (Plut. *Cat. mai.* 1.3). Being young aristocrats, the *equites* were enthusiastic and brave, but better at making a headlong charge on the battlefield than patrolling or scouting. This was a reflection of the lack of a real cavalry tradition in Rome, as well as the fact that the *equites* included the sons of many senators, eager to make a name for courage and so help their future political careers. Before being eligible for political office in Rome, a man had to have served for ten campaigns with the army.

The allied cavalry force was generally two or three times larger than that provided by Roman citizens. These horsemen were organized in *turmae*, probably the same strength as the Roman, and were presumably also from the wealthiest strata of society. This is certainly suggested by Livy's references to 300 young men of the noblest Campanian families serving in Sicilia, and to the young noblemen from Tarentum who served at the battles of Lake Trasimene and Cannae (Liv. 23.7.2, 24.13.1). The cavalry was commanded,

ABOVE LEFT
Montefortino helmet type A (Museo civico archeologico di Bologna, inv. 28233) of bronze, from the Necropoli Benacci, tomba 953, turn of the 3rd century BC. This pattern of helmet probably arrived in the Italian peninsula with the Senonian Gauls at the end of the 5th century BC (Cascarino 2007: 104), and it was quickly adopted by the Etruscans, Latins and Samnites. (© Esther Carré)

ABOVE RIGHT
Montefortino helmet type A (Volterra, Museo Guarnacci, inv. MG 9737), from an Etruscan burial. The Montefortino was distinguished by its bulbous pointed shape and integral knob on the top, which serves as a crest, its holder and protruding neck guard. (quinet [Thomas Quine], CC BY-SA 2.0 https://creativecommons.org/licenses/by-sa/2.0, via Wikimedia Commons)

Terracotta attachment (New York, Metropolitan Museum of Art, inv. 12.236.5) in the form of Italic horsemen in combat, from a funnel jar of Magna Graecia origin, late 3rd–early 2nd century BC. While most of Rome's cavalry were provided for by the Latin/Italian *socii*, they were commanded by Roman *praefecti equitum*. The fallen horseman wears a bronze or linen corselet with *pteruges*, while his victorious opponent is in a short tunic, *chiton*. As well as their round-bossed shields, the horsemen originally carried one or two light spears or javelins. (Rogers Fund, 1912, Metropolitan Museum of Art)

at least from the 2nd century BC, by Roman *praefecti equitum*, presumably with local *decuriones* and *optiones* at *turma* level. Like their citizen counterparts, as well as having a higher social status, allied horsemen were much better paid than those serving as foot soldiers (Polyb. 6.39.14–15).

Polybios (6.25.3–8) discusses the changes in the Roman cavalry in some detail, emphasizing that the *equites* were now armed in 'the Greek fashion', namely bronze helmet, stiff linen corselet, strong circular shield, long spear, complete with a butt-spike, and sword, but he observes that formerly (perhaps up to the Pyrrhic War) they had lacked body armour and had carried only a short spear and a small ox-hide shield, which was too light for adequate protection at close quarters and tended to rot in the rain. Polybios actually compares its shape to a type of round-bossed cake, namely those that are commonly used in sacrifices. This earlier shield may be the type shown on the Tarentine 'horsemen' coins of the early 4th century BC, with a flat rim and convex centre (Fields 2008B: 28, 61).

The sword carried by the *equites* appears to have been the *gladius Hispaniensis*. If true, then the *gladius* used by the *equites* may well have been a little longer than that of the infantry. Livy refers to 'arms torn away, shoulders and all, heads separated from bodies with the necks completely severed, and stomachs ripped open' (31.34.4).

Contrary to popular belief, the lack of stirrups was not a major handicap to ancient horsemen, especially those 'born in the saddle' like the Numidians. Roman cavalry of the time was perhaps already using the padded saddle with four horns made by internal bronze stiffeners, which provides an admirably firm seat. Like most equestrian equipment, it was almost certainly of Celtic origin as it is depicted on the Gundestrop cauldron, which pre-dates the 1st century BC.

When a rider's weight was lowered onto this type of saddle the four tall horns, *cornicule*, closed around and gripped his thighs, but they did not inhibit free movement to the same extent as a modern pommel and cantle designed for rider comfort and safety. This was especially important to spear- and sword-carrying cavalry favoured by the Romans, whose drill called for some almost acrobatic changes of position. In an age that did not have the stirrup, the adoption of the four-horned saddle, as experimental work has shown (Hyland 1990: 130–4), allowed the horseman to effectively launch a missile while skirmishing, or confidently use both hands to wield his shield and spear (or sword) in a whirling mêlée. The main function of its wooden frame was to protect the horse's spine from shock during a charge, and its design transferred the rider's weight to the animal's flanks. The saddle was secured with a breast strap, haunch straps and breeching, and a girth that passed through a woollen saddlecloth under which a smaller cloth of fur may have been placed to give the horse greater protection from chaffing.

Though aristocratic horsemen, *equites*, served in the legions, the Romans – unlike the Numidians – did not have a tradition of horsemanship. Most of their cavalry, therefore, were provided for by the Latin/Italian *socii*. This Alabaster cinerary urn (Volterra, Museo Etrusco, inv. MG278), 2nd century BC, shows an Etruscan horseman wearing a short mail shirt with shoulder doubling and *pteruges*. He also wears an Etrusco-Corinthian helmet. He is armed with a sturdy spear, which possibly carries a butt-spike. (© Esther Carré)

Battle tactics

Polybios does not offer his readers an account of the legion in battle, but there are a number of combat descriptions both in his own work and that of Livy. However, very few accounts describe tactics in detail; a contemporary Roman (or Greek) audience would take much for granted. Even so, the legion would usually approach the enemy in its standard battle formation, the *triplex acies*, which was based around the triple line of *hastati*, *principes* and *triarii*, with the *velites* forming a screen in front. To repeat, each of these three lines consisted of ten maniples.[6] When deployed, each maniple may have been separated from its lateral neighbour by the width of its own frontage (*c.* 18m), though this is still a matter of some debate. Livy tells us that the maniples were 'a small distance apart' (8.8.5), which does not really help us a great deal. Moreover, the maniples of *hastati*, *principes* and *triarii* were staggered, with the more seasoned *principes* covering the gaps of the *hastati* in front, and likewise the veteran *triarii* covering those of the

---

6 At one point of his narrative Sallust (50.2) actually uses the term *cohortes* and not *manipuli*. It is uncertain whether or not this is an inconsistency on Sallust's part, for Marius is supposed to have introduced this change after the Jugurthine War, not during it.

A pair of Roman *gladii* (Calahorra, Museo de la romanización), 3rd–1st century BC. The *gladius Hispaniensis* was developed from a Celtiberian cut-and-thrust sword and allowed legionaries to fight side by side with *scuta* taking the blows of the longer swords of their foes. The *gladius* was borne high on the right hip, its scabbard employing a four-ring suspension system. Legionaries were trained to thrust using a straight backsword. The thrust usually inflicted mortal wounds, whereas even multiple cuts were seldom fatal. (Artistosteles, CC BY-SA 4.0 https://creativecommons.org/licenses/by-sa/4.0, via Wikimedia Commons)

principes. This battle formation is conveniently called by those who study the Roman Army the *quincunx*, from the five dots on a dice cube.

As was customary in battle, the *velites*, strung out before the *quincunx*, delivered the opening shots in an attempt to disorganize and unsettle enemy formations with a rapid hail of javelins. This done, they scurried through the gaps between the maniples of the *hastati* and made their way to the rear. The maniples of the *hastati* now re-formed to close the gaps, either by each maniple extending its frontage, thus giving individuals more room in which to handle their weapons, or, if the maniple was drawn up two centuries deep, the *centurio posterior* would move his *centuria* to the left and forward, thus running out and forming up alongside the *centuria* of the *centurio prior* in the line itself (Keppie 1998: 38–9).

The *hastati* would discharge their *pila*, throwing first their light and then their heavy *pila*, some 15m from the enemy. The term *hastati* should be taken to mean armed with throwing spears, namely *pila*, instead of thrusting ones. This is after all the sense it bears out in our earliest surviving example of it, in Ennius' line '*hastati spargunt hasti*', '*hastati* who hurl *hasti*' (*Annales* fr. 284 Vahlen), and their name probably reflects a time when they alone used *pila*.

During the confusion caused by this hail of *pila*, which could be devastating, the *hastati* drew their swords and, said Polybios, 'charged the enemy yelling their war cry and clashing their weapons against their shields as is their custom' (15.12.8, cf. 1.34.2). He also says the Romans formed up in a much looser formation than did other contemporary close-order infantry (Polyb. 18.30.6–8), adding this was necessary to use the sword and for the soldier to defend himself all round with his shield. This implies the legionary was essentially an individual fighter, a swordsman. Yet the elder Cato, who served during the Second Punic War as an *eques* and a *quaestor*, always maintained that a soldier's bearing, confidence and the ferociousness of his war cry were more important than his actual skill with a blade (Plut. *Cat. mai.* 1.4).

In his brief description of the *gladius Hispaniensis*, Polybios evidently says the sword was 'worn high on the right thigh' so as to be clear of the legs – a vertically held scabbard would normally be impractical for walking let alone for fighting – adding that it was an excellent weapon 'for thrusting, and both of its edges cut effectually, as the blade is very strong and firm' (6.23.6–7). The wearing of the sword on the right side goes back to the Iberians, and before them, to the Celts. The sword was the weapon of the high-status warrior, and to carry one was to display a symbol of rank and prestige. It was probably for cultural reasons alone, therefore, that the Celts carried the long slashing sword on the right side. Usually, a sword was worn on the left, the side covered by the shield, which obviously meant the weapon was hidden from plain sight.

If, at this early date, the legionary already carried his sword on the right-hand side suspended by a sword (waist) belt, it would not be for any cultural reason. As opposed to a scabbard-slide, the four-ring suspension system on his scabbard enabled the legionary to draw his weapon quickly with the right hand, an asset in close-quarter combat. In view of its relatively short blade, inverting the hand to grasp the hilt and pushing the pommel forward drew the *gladius* with ease. With its sharp point and four-ring suspension arrangement, the Delos sword, firmly dated to 69 BC, shows all the characteristics of the *gladius Hispaniensis* described a century earlier by Polybios. Another such example is the *gladius Hispaniensis* from Mouriès (*département* Bouches-du-Rhône), found in a tomb in association with a group of pottery and metal artefacts. This assembly can be dated to around 100 BC (Bishop and Coulston 1993: 53; Feugère 1993: 79), a time when the Romans were dealing with the Cimbri and the Teutones: the battles of Arausio (105 BC) and Aquae Sextiae (102 BC) were fought nearby (Fields 2023).

Polybios, in an excursion dedicated to the comparison between Roman and Macedonian military equipment and tactical formations, says the following: 'According to the Roman methods of fighting each man makes his movements individually: not only does he defend his body with his long shield, constantly moving it to meet a threatened blow, but he uses his sword both for cutting and for thrusting' (Polyb. 18.30.6). What we are witnessing here is the intelligent use, by a swordsman, of the sword. It appears, therefore, that the tactical doctrine commonly associated with the Roman legion of the Principate was already in place during Polybios' day. We know from the archaeological record that the *gladius* of the Principate ('Pompeii' type) was a remarkably light and well-balanced weapon that was capable of making blindingly fast attacks, and was suitable for both cuts and thrusts. However, Tacitus (b. *c.* AD 56) and Vegetius (*fl. c.* AD 385) lay great stress on the *gladius* being employed by the legionary for thrusting rather than slashing: as Vegetius rightly points out, 'a slash-cut, whatever its force, seldom kills' (1.12), and so a thrust was certainly more likely to deliver the fatal wound.

The use of the thrust also meant the legionary kept most of his torso well covered, and thus protected, by his *scutum*. The latter, having absorbed the attack of his antagonist, was now punched into the face of the opponent as the legionary stepped forward to jab with his *gladius*. The *scutum* was used both defensively and offensively to deflect blows and hammer into the opponent's shield or body to create openings. As he stood with his left foot forward, a legionary could get much of his body weight behind this punch. Added to this was the considerable weight of the *scutum* itself. He would then jab his enemy in the belly with the razor-sharp point of his *gladius* (Tac. *Ann.* 2.14, 21, 14.36, *Hist.* 2.42, *Agr.* 36.2). In short: with *pila* whistling, *gladii* jabbing, *scuta* punching, the legionaries made carnage.

Preferably, the *hastati* fought the main enemy line to a standstill, but if they were rebuffed, or lost momentum, the *principes* advanced into the combat zone and the process was repeated. Hand-to-hand fighting was physically strenuous and emotionally draining, and the skill of a Roman commander lay in committing his second and third lines at the right time. Obviously, the survivors of the *hastati* and the *principes* now reinforced the *triarii* if it came down to a final trial of strength. The phrase '*inde rem ad triarios redisse*' ('the last resource is in the *triarii*') (Liv. 8.8.9) passed into the Latin tongue as a description of a desperate situation. Victory would eventually go to the side that endured the stress of staying so close to the enemy for the longest and was still able to urge enough of its men forward to renew the fighting. It was the inherent flexibility of the manipular system that made the legion a formidable battlefield opponent. In Polybios' measured analysis:

> The order of battle used by the Roman army is very difficult to break through, since it allows every man to fight both individually and collectively; the effect is to offer a formation that can present a front in any direction, since the maniples that are nearest to the point where danger threatens wheel in order to meet it. The arms they carry both give protection and also instil great confidence into the men, because of the size of the shields and the strength of the swords, which can withstand repeated blows. All these factors make the Romans formidable antagonists in battle and very hard to overcome (Polyb. 15.15.7–10).

Contemporary Hellenistic armies, for instance, preferred to deepen their phalanx rather than form troops into a second line, and made little use of reserves, as the commander's role was usually to charge at the head of his cavalry. The Roman system, on the other hand, allowed fresh men to be fed into the fighting line, renewing its impetus and leading a surge forward, which might well have been enough to break a wearying enemy.

In battle, physical endurance is of the utmost importance and all soldiers in close contact with danger become emotionally if not physically exhausted as the battle proceeds. It is estimated that in antiquity a soldier, wielding spear, javelin or sword and protecting himself with shield and body armour, was effective during a period of up to 30 minutes in constant combat (Gabriel and Metz 1991: 42–3). At that point, both physical and emotional exhaustion took over. Battle tactics prior to those of the Romans did not allow for the swift replacement of reserves and the relief of the front line. When writing of ancient warfare, Colonel Ardent du Picq, the French military theorist, notes the great value of the Roman system was that it kept only those units that were necessary at the point of combat and the rest 'outside the immediate sphere of moral tension' (1946: 53). The legion, organized into separate battle lines, was able to hold one-half to two-thirds of its men outside the danger zone – the zone of demoralization – in which the remaining half or third was engaged.

The greater part of a soldier's time is spent waiting for something to happen. He has little to think about, but his commander much. Obviously, the skill of a Roman commander lay not in sharing the dangers with his men

LEGIO PRIMA GERMANICA equipped and armed as a veteran legionary, a *triarios*. The third line of the manipular legion still wielded the *hasta*, a weapon not for throwing but for thrusting. He is equipped with a long, iron mail shirt and Italic bronze greaves. He carries an Italic *scutum* with metal binding top and bottom and a metal boss plate reinforcing the wooden spindle boss. He is gripping a *hasta* with a large, socketed iron spearhead, and a bronze butt-spike, a weapon of last resort if his *hasta* snapped. A *gladius Hispaniensis* is carried in its scabbard high on the right hip. (Photograph courtesy of Graham Sumner)

Mars, god of war, on the Altar of Domitius Ahenobarbus (Paris, Musée du Louvre, inv. Ma 975), dressed in the uniform of a senior officer. Looking more Hellenistic than Roman, he wears a short, decorated muscle cuirass equipped with two rows of fringed *pteruges*, greaves and a crested Etrusco-Corinthian helmet. A peculiar and perverted development of the closed Greek Corinthian helmet commonly worn by hoplites, this pattern was worn on top of the head jockey fashion while preserving for decorative purposes the now redundant eyeholes and nasal guard of the original. He also has a circular shield, a spear and a sword, which he carries on the left side. The knotted sash around his waist denotes his rank. (© Esther Carré)

but in committing his second and third lines at the right moments. Left too late then the fighting line might buckle and break. Too soon and the value of adding fresh soldiers to the mêlée might be wasted. He therefore needed to influence what he read as critical incidents or phases of the battle. Even if simple in concept, this manipular system depended on its success in the commander's touch and timing.

THE CAMPAIGN

Maxima pars urbis exusta cum aede Matris Magnae. Lacte per triduum pluit, hostiisque expiatum maioribus. Iugurthinum bellum exortum. / A great part of the city [Rome] was burned, along with the temple of Magna Mater. It rained milk for three days, and the expiation was done with full-grown sacrificial victims. The Jugurthine War began.
Iulius Obsequens, *Prodigiorum liber* 39

FAMILY DRAMA

In 118 BC, the dying Micipsa bequeathed his kingdom to his two legitimate sons, Adherbal and Hiempsal, and to his younger brother's illegitimate son, Jugurtha (*B Iug.* 9.2). And so it was that Jugurtha put to death first one then the other of his less belligerent cousins and made himself master of Numidia (r. 112–106 BC). In 116 BC, following the murder of Hiempsal, Adherbal came before the Senate to plead his case against Jugurtha. On the other hand, to lay his side of the matter before the Senate, Jugurtha opted to act through the agency of envoys – *legati*, as Sallust calls them. Adherbal was clearly the injured party; yet what followed was a senatorial debate in which Sallust says the flatterers of Jugurtha, apparently bribed, along with the majority of the house, praised him and derided Adherbal, implying he was the aggressor (*B Iug.* 15.1–4). A senatorial commission consisting of ten envoys was then dispatched to Numidia and divided the kingdom between Adherbal and Jugurtha. The commission would investigate and its decision would be considered logical and final, with no room for flagrant bribery.

Dynastic squabbles of this nature had never been uncommon among the Numidians, and it was just such a quarrel that had first prompted Masinissa to seek aid from Publius Cornelius Scipio in his struggle against Syphax. Stories of senatorial corruption, dreadful in truth and much exaggerated in the telling, had been circulating for some time. But was this in fact the case? To answer this, we need to look at the following key points.

For Sallust's claim of corruption to make sense, the bipartite division of Numidia should have been in favour of Jugurtha – 'richer in territory and population' (*B Iug.* 16.5). This is misinformation, for Adherbal received the major towns and ports of the kingdom, including the capital Cirta (Constantine, Algeria). Actually, it could be argued that sustained lobbying and some discriminating bribery on Adherbal's behalf had helped secure this result.

In truth, Jugurtha's share was much less valuable in terms of real estate and, more to the point, he had been shoved over to the western half of Numidia. This clearly implies that Rome saw him as a potential troublemaker, and so established him furthest from *provincia Africa*. In effect, Adherbal's half of the kingdom was to act as a buffer between Roman territory and that of Jugurtha.

There was no *raison d'être* for Rome to directly intervene in Numidia, which after all was *not* part of the empire. For this reason, the Senate achieved a workable settlement through diplomacy. After all, diplomacy, rather than conquest, was the *modus operandi* of Rome's imperial statecraft. As far as the Senate was concerned, the sensible course was to leave the squabbling princes to stew in their own juice. It was their row. Good sense was against meddling, so the senators decided not to. Yet on this occasion, senatorial good sense was to be no match for pride, prejudice and vested interests. It was a bad start, and things got worse.

COUSINS' WAR

In 112 BC, Jugurtha invaded Adherbal's half of the kingdom, 'taking many mortals captive along with their livestock, as well as other plunder, set fire to buildings and raided a great number of places with his cavalry' (*B Iug.* 20.3). The hope was to provoke Adherbal into counterattacks and thereby provide Jugurtha with a suitable excuse for making open war upon him. But Adherbal would not be provoked. He put his faith in Roman power and sent envoys to Rome. The Senate responded by dispatching two delegations to Numidia to inform the princes they must disarm and settle their differences according to the law.

Sallust claims that both these delegations were 'soft' on Jugurtha, and his explanation is simple: bribery (e.g. *B Iug.* 13.5–8, 15.1, 3, 15.5–16.1, 3–4, 20.1). That, of course, suits Sallust's purpose. Again, however, let us look at the facts behind the larger issues facing the Senate at the time.

Conical-style iron helmet (Constantine, Musée national Cirta) from the Mausoleum Soumaā d'el-Khroub, *c.* 120 BC. It has a projection at the rear to protect the neck, and ears embossed at the sides (to ward off harm?). Although this is a Numidian example, the conical-style helmet was much favoured in earlier eastern empires (*viz.* Neo-Assyrian, Achaemenid Persian) and was probably introduced into the northern African littoral by the Phoenicians: examples are shown, though in crude triangular form, on Punic stelae. (Jona Lendering/Livius.org/CC0 1.0 Universal)

Sallust implies it was discreditable that the envoys of the first delegation were three young and inexperienced men (*B Iug.* 21.4). His comments overlook the fact that there was a reason why the Senate sent the young men in the first place, and it has nothing, or almost nothing, to do with appeasing Jugurtha. It was because such men were invariably the sons of senators, many of whom were gaining valuable political experience for the first time. Contrary to Sallust, this was customary diplomatic practice.

Marcus Aemilius Scaurus (*cos.* 115 BC), the *princeps senatus* (*B Iug.* 25.4, Plin. 8.223), 'chief of the Senate' (in voting, his opinion was asked first), advocated going to war on behalf of Adherbal, but the supporters of Jugurtha – for whatever motive – prevented it. He headed the second delegation of 'elder nobles' (*B Iug.* 25.4). For Cicero (e.g. *pro Murena* 16, 36, *Brut.* 112, 136), Scaurus was the paramount statesman and master of civic wisdom, never named except for praise. Sallust has much to say of pretence and inconsistency in politics, and so finds Scaurus rather objectionable, as he evidently despises Cicero: both were prepared to change their policies and adapt themselves to current circumstances. For Sallust, Scaurus was cunning and unscrupulous, always making sure he was never associated with a losing cause (*B Iug.* 15.4–5). Sallust, a plain-spoken person who tended to see affairs of state in shades of black and white, paints Scaurus as an archetypal *nobilis*. Yet even today the willingness to compromise is essential to successful statesmanship.

A Roman army in Macedonia, under Caius Porcius Cato (*cos.* 114 BC), was of late trounced by the Thracian Scordisci, and so Rome could not afford to get itself embroiled in another war. Worse still, Rome had to face a grave emergency on its northern frontiers, provoked by the recent migrations of the Cimbri and Teutones, Cnaeus Papirius Carbo (*cos.* 113 BC) having crossed the Alpes Iuliae only to be routed by the Cimbri. The Numidian situation therefore was the least of the Senate's worries, and some senators probably would have preferred to have ignored the problems of Numidia in the hope that they would solve them themselves. It was not to be.

Overly confident – he did not hold all the cards right now, but certainly held a lot of them – Jugurtha eventually risked his position by overplaying his ambitions and invading the territory Rome had allotted to Adherbal. Adherbal had previously sent envoys to remonstrate with his adoptive brother, but to no effect. Jugurtha took this parleying as a sign of weakness and began the war in earnest. Jugurtha almost certainly believed he could defy Rome because of its current conflict with the Cimbri and the Teutones, which was much closer to home.

With little or no option, Adherbal raised an army and reluctantly met Jugurtha outside his capital, Cirta. The two armies approached each other but as it was late in the day did not engage. During the small hours of the following morning, however, while it was still dark, Jugurtha attacked Adherbal's camp and completely routed his drowsy army. Adherbal escaped in the confusion with a small mounted force and fled to Cirta, where he was saved from capture by resident Italians, Romans included, traders (*negotiatores*) to be exact, the town being an important centre for the African grain trade. They obstructed the hot pursuit from the walls, undoubtedly with missile weapons, and had it not been for this, 'the war between the two kings would have been begun and finished on a single day' (*B Iug.* 21.2). A senatorial commission arrived to mediate, followed by a second, but to no avail.

Jugurtha thereupon settled into besieging Cirta, a fortress squatting atop a ravine-girt promontory, with mantlets, towers and rams (*B Iug.* 21.3). If this was truly the case, then such an approach demonstrated his army was far more technologically sophisticated than might be expected from an out-of-the-way semi-desert kingdom. However, with its all-encompassing precipitous ravines, save for a narrow isthmus, Cirta could not be besieged by the usual means. Sallust understood Cirta was besieged, and had therefore assumed Jugurtha employed the conventional besieging techniques of *vallum*, *fossa* and the rest: despite his personal connection and residence in Numidia, Sallust shows little or no attempt to make use of information he might have gleaned by autopsy. Having served at Numantia, Jugurtha would have learned about *obsidio*, literally 'blockade', whereby supplies are blocked so as to starve the enemy into submission, and in all probability, he applied this time-consuming approach at Cirta. Contrary to Sallust, Adherbal was hemmed in by the brutal vigilance of Jugurtha.

The siege was to drag on for some five months. During this period, a pantomime of negotiations was conducted between Jugurtha and Rome, the king blatantly ignoring instructions from the two senatorial missions to desist and disarm. Sallust believed that Cirta held out so long principally because of the valour of the resident Italians (*B Iug.* 22.2, 26.1, 3). Even if this is a case of patriotic exaggeration, the Italians, fearing for their own safety, finally prevailed upon Adherbal to surrender his capital on the terms that he would be spared and that the Senate would then sort the mess out. Adherbal was rightly dubious, but submitted to the Italians' pressure. Adherbal's assessment of the situation was more astute than that of the Italians. Cirta capitulated, and Adherbal was tortured to death. That was not all. Jugurtha ordered the slaughter of all the Italians in Cirta who had taken up arms and shared in its defence, an indiscriminate killing as callous and spiteful as may be found even in Numidian history.

Cirta, Algeria, the Numidian capital after the Second Punic War. Situated on a spectacular promontory girt with precipitous ravines on all sides, except for a narrow isthmus. Punic settlers (from Carthage) had established a settlement here around 300 BC called Kirtha, 'the city'. In 113–112 BC, Jugurtha besieged what was then Adherbal's capital, eventually forcing it to capitulate, slaughtering its inhabitants and the resident Italian traders settled there. Adherbal was captured and soon after murdered. (EL Hacene Boulkroune, CC BY-SA 4.0 https://creativecommons.org/licenses/by-sa/4.0, via Wikimedia Commons)

In all conflicts there are tipping points. Thresholds that are crossed. Moments of not looking back. After the massacre of the Italians at Cirta, something profound changed. Jugurtha had gone too far: the Senate as a matter of course decided on war. In spite of, according to Sallust, Jugurtha's lavish use of bribery, the senators were bent on punishing the Numidian king for his blatant acts of aggression against a treaty ally. Livy (*Per.* 64), alternatively, makes the murder of Adherbal the reason for war, there being no mention of the slaughter at Cirta. Adherbal, after all, had been under the protection of the Roman people. Whatever the reason, doubtless his success at Cirta had convinced the Senate Jugurtha would now have to be taken seriously. And so a full-scale war in Africa was shaping up.

BESTIA TAKES COMMAND

Rationally, with the massacre of Italians at Cirta, the Senate had no option but to accept the *fait accompli* and take direct action against Jugurtha. Not only had this African massacre knocked away the prop on which the peace of Numidia rested, but also, as the tendrils of empire, it must have confirmed for all the Italians (and Romans) in Africa that they depended on the credibility of Rome's reach to intervene. With that, Lucius Calpurnius Bestia, one of the consuls of 111 BC, had Numidia allotted as his province (i.e. area of operation); at this time, it was quite usual for a consul to be sent to a foreign command during his year of office.

Bestia landed in Numidia, displayed Roman arms, and dragged Jugurtha to the peace table (*B Iug.* 30.1–3). Sallust smells graft and degeneracy – Bestia had energy, a keen intelligence and skill in warfare, but all these noble qualities were hampered by his greed for profit (*B Iug.* 28.5). He had selected as his staff of *legati* men of birth who would likely cover up his transgressions – among these was Marcus Aemilius Scaurus (*B Iug.* 28.4). That, for Sallust at least, was sufficient enough to denounce Bestia – his campaign began with victory, but was undone by bribery. But let us consider the following points first before we do the same.

With two *legiones* and an equal number of Latin/Italian *alae*, Bestia could have clobbered Jugurtha in a short, sharp campaign, or so say the armchair strategists – Sallust, to his credit, knew Africa and knew warfare. However, Bestia's objective was to pacify Jugurtha while Rome dealt with the Thracian Scordisci who were rampaging through the province of Macedonia, and it is difficult to disagree with the Senate's determination to try and deal with this closer-to-home threat. 'War', suggested James Wolfe before storming the Heights of Abraham, 'is an option of difficulties', and the Senate certainly has its fair share of difficulties to choose from.

The peace negotiation, by which Jugurtha accepted what the Senate formally recognized as an unconditional surrender to the faith of the Roman people (*in fidem populi Romani se dare deditio*), made perfect sense. Accordingly, Jugurtha acknowledged the supremacy of Rome, paid a modest war indemnity, and handed over 30 war elephants (though he may have kept others: he later had at least 44) along with a good many head of cattle and horses. In return, he was installed as the sole king of Numidia. With this diplomatic compromise, both sides gained and the war might had ended here.

Numidian theatre of war

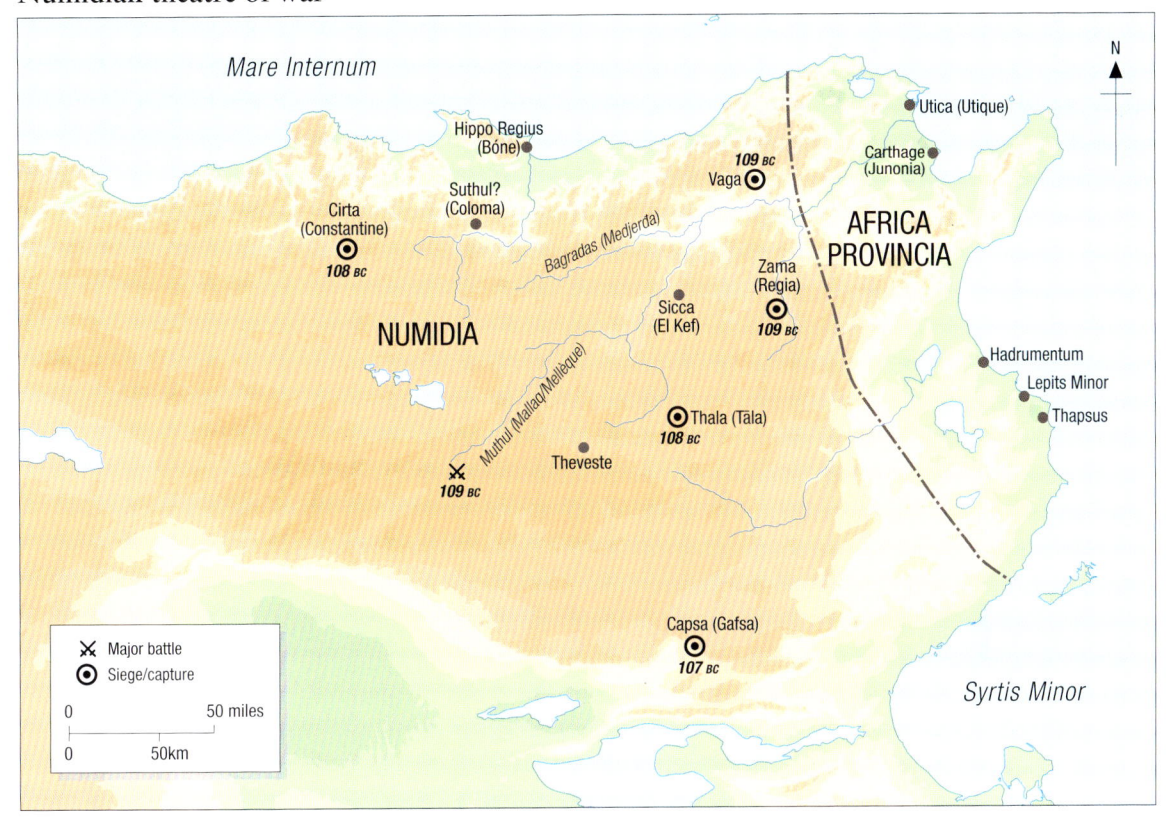

Naturally, from the standpoint of Bestia, it was better to bring the Numidian campaign to a profitable conclusion while he remained in office, despite Jugurtha's continued freedom. Though Jugurtha was summoned under diplomatic immunity to inquiry in Rome, the Senate, seeing no reason to fight the king to the bitter end, appears to have acquiesced. But the peace was illusory. Jugurtha was still intent on tightening his total control over a unified Numidia. In the *Bellum Iugurthinum*, Sallust expounds two contests: the one waged against Jugurtha, the other against the *nobilitas*. For him, Jugurtha's unconditional surrender was a euphemism of huge proportions: it neither stopped the war nor did it bring peace.

SPURIUS POSTUMIUS TAKES COMMAND

Jugurtha had another cousin, Massiva, a son of Gulussa, who had wisely fled to Rome after the fall of Cirta and the murder of Adherbal. Massiva had fallen in with Spurius Postumius Albinus, one of the consuls of 110 BC. Spurius Postumius was, as Sallust says, 'eager to conduct a war' (*avidus belli gerundi*: B Iug. 35.3), and so persuaded Massiva, who, after all, was a legitimate grandson of Masinissa, to claim Jugurtha's throne from the Senate. Now, Spurius Postumius was to replace Bestia in command of the army in Numidia, and he reasoned that by placing Massiva on the Numidian throne, he would have a client running the kingdom. It must have seemed a very sweet proposition.

Numidian bronze coin (Constantine, Musée national Cirta). Obverse: bust of Gulussa, c. 145 BC. The Numidian kings were careful to cultivate the image of the model Hellenistic monarch through their coinage: a diadem is bound around Gulussa's hair, a typically Hellenistic symbol of kinship. He was the second son of Masinissa, brother of Micipsa and Mastanabal. Gulussa's son was Massiva, who was assassinated on the orders of his cousin Jugurtha while in Rome. (Jona Lendering/Livius.org/CC0 1.0 Universal)

Jugurtha was alarmed at the possibility, so he turned to the usual Jugurthine solution: murder. With characteristic rashness, he ordered his confidant, Bomilcar, to hire out Massiva's murder. It was to be done secretly, if possible, but in any case, it was to be done, and done quickly. The wishes of the unscrupulous king were duly obeyed and Massiva was accordingly liquidated. The deed itself, however, was bungled in that one of the assassins was caught and persuaded by the authorities to confess all. The Senate had no choice but to order Jugurtha to quit Rome immediately. The war was renewed.

There are those infamous words that Sallust puts into the mouth of Jugurtha as he is leaving Rome: 'A city for sale and soon to perish, if it finds a buyer!' (*B Iug.* 35.10, repeated almost verbatim in App. *Num.* fr. 1 and Flor. 1.36.18). In spite of Jugurtha's lavish use of bribery, how fair this accusation is we cannot say with certainty, but it is probably an exaggeration. It does support Sallust's analysis of Rome: everything in his account has led us to believe that the city was indeed corrupt and rushing to its destruction. What is certain, however, is the Senate had decided that Jugurtha was to be crushed whatever the cost.

The ignominious surrender of the consul's brother, *pro praetore* Aulus Postumius Albinus, whom Spurius had left in command while he returned to Rome to oversee the disruptive consular elections, and the peace concluded on Jugurtha's terms, were inevitably repudiated by the Senate (*B Iug.* 39.3, Liv. *Per.* 64). And thereby hangs a miserable tale. Sallust may smell the stink of senatorial corruption everywhere, but while the consul was in Rome, his brother had indulged himself in a rather rash foray: his objective was Suthul (not identified), the town where Jugurtha had deposited his treasury (Oros. 5.15.6), and where Aulus Postumius '[C]ame to hope for either finishing the war [*spem ... conficundi belli*] or obtaining a bribe from the king because of the fear the army inspired in him' (*B Iug.* 37.3).

Aulus Postumius found the town on the edge of a steep hill above a marshy valley, which had been flooded by winter rains and become a lake (*B Iug.* 37.4). Undaunted, he set about reducing the place, building a rampart outside the town. In the meantime, Jugurtha turned to the most useful tool in his armoury: trickery. And so the *pro praetore* was lured into a trap by the king, having lifted the siege and followed blindly the Numidian army into increasingly remoter parts of Numidia.

Jugurtha's defining trait was his audacity. Once the Roman army was satisfactorily isolated, he sprung his trap. In the dead of night, he suddenly surrounded the Roman marching camp, and gave the signal for the Ligurum *cohors* and the two *turmae* of Thracians he had managed to suborn to make their move. At the same time, the chief centurion of the Third Legion (*B Iug.* 38.6), who had also been turned, opened the gate he was in charge of and allowed a Numidian party into the sleeping camp. With his camp at least badly mauled, at most overrun – a classic example of coming up against an enemy who used novel tactics and strategies on unfamiliar terrain – Aulus Postumius was forced to capitulate. The following morning Jugurtha was quite prepared to let the Romans go – for a price. Borrowing an old Italic (not Numidian) custom, Aulus Postumius and his defeated men were made to file under the yoke and agreed to quit Numidia within ten days. The very symbol of defeat, the yoke was a frame made from two spears stuck in the ground with a third one lashed horizontally at a height that compelled the soldiers of Rome, who were disarmed and clad only in their woollen tunics, to crouch down underneath. The alternative was simple: 'starvation and the sword' (*B Iug.* 38.9). To be trounced by a pack of 'naked unskilled savages' made this humiliation all the greater. Now there could be no more compromise.

Jugurtha's only undisputed victory over a Roman army was won through trickery and finalized by a trade. It is enough for us to point out that imputations of bribery, gladly taken up by Sallust, do not have to be invoked to explain Aulus Albinus' incompetent and calamitous performance. The senatorial general was just that, hapless and incompetent, and perhaps greedy. On top of that, the compromising of their marching camp was a drain on his men's already low morale. It is possible to be sorry for Aulus Postumius. In one night, his world tumbled. Yet, the folly of Aulus Postumius abolished all hopes of an accommodation between Jugurtha and Rome: the knavish king was to be taken dead or alive. For this reason, the next two commanders were to devote their efforts in Numidia not so much to the conquest of territory as to the relentless pursuit of an individual.

Clearly, Numidia was an evolving nightmare. After the two unsuccessful attempts to crush Jugurtha, the Senate dispatched the quixotic but competent Quintus Caecilius Metellus against him. The Caecilii Metelli were the most prominent family in Rome at this time and their honorific cognomens (*Delmaticus*, *Macedonicus*, *Balearicus*)[7] fittingly serve as a key to Rome's expansion during the 2nd century BC.

METELLUS TAKES COMMAND

Every army, like any other body of men, is subtly pervaded by the quality of its commander, even if the rank and file rarely glimpse him. So, when the commander does not command, the army cannot obey. Complacency, the mother of all fiends, creeps in, and then it is a downward slope. All becomes confusion. Yet united in profound kinship with their commander, the soldiers respond with uncompromising loyalty. They will obey every order. They will accompany him far and wide, into grave danger, into death. When soldiers

---

[7] Quintus Caecilius Metellus Macedonicus (*cos.* 143 BC), Quintus Caecilius Metellus Balearicus (*cos.* 123 BC), Quintus Caecilius Metellus Delmaticus (*cos.* 119 BC), to be followed by Quintus Caecilius Metellus Numidicus (*cos.* 109 BC), and Quintus Caecilius Metellus Creticus (*cos.* 69 BC).

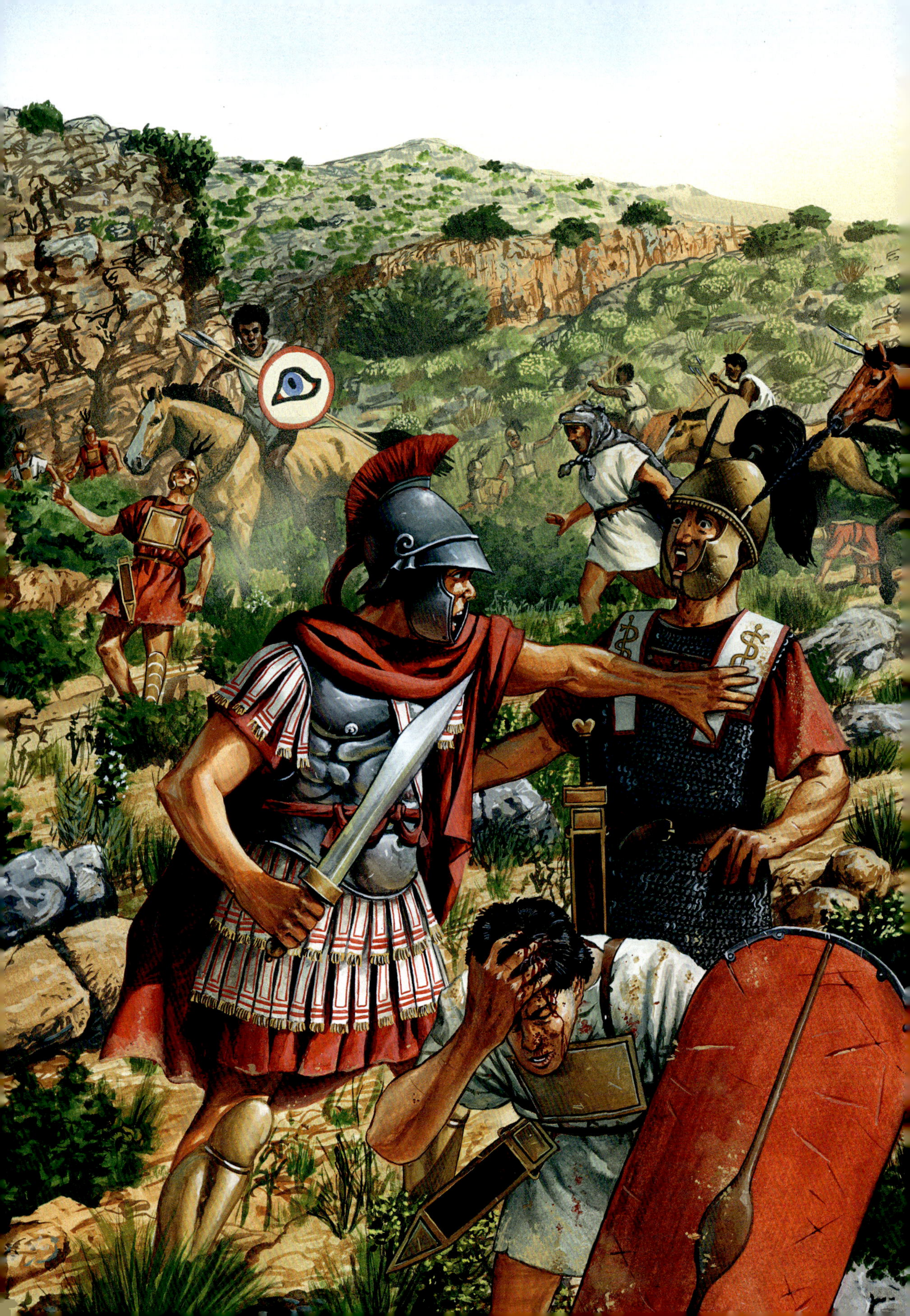

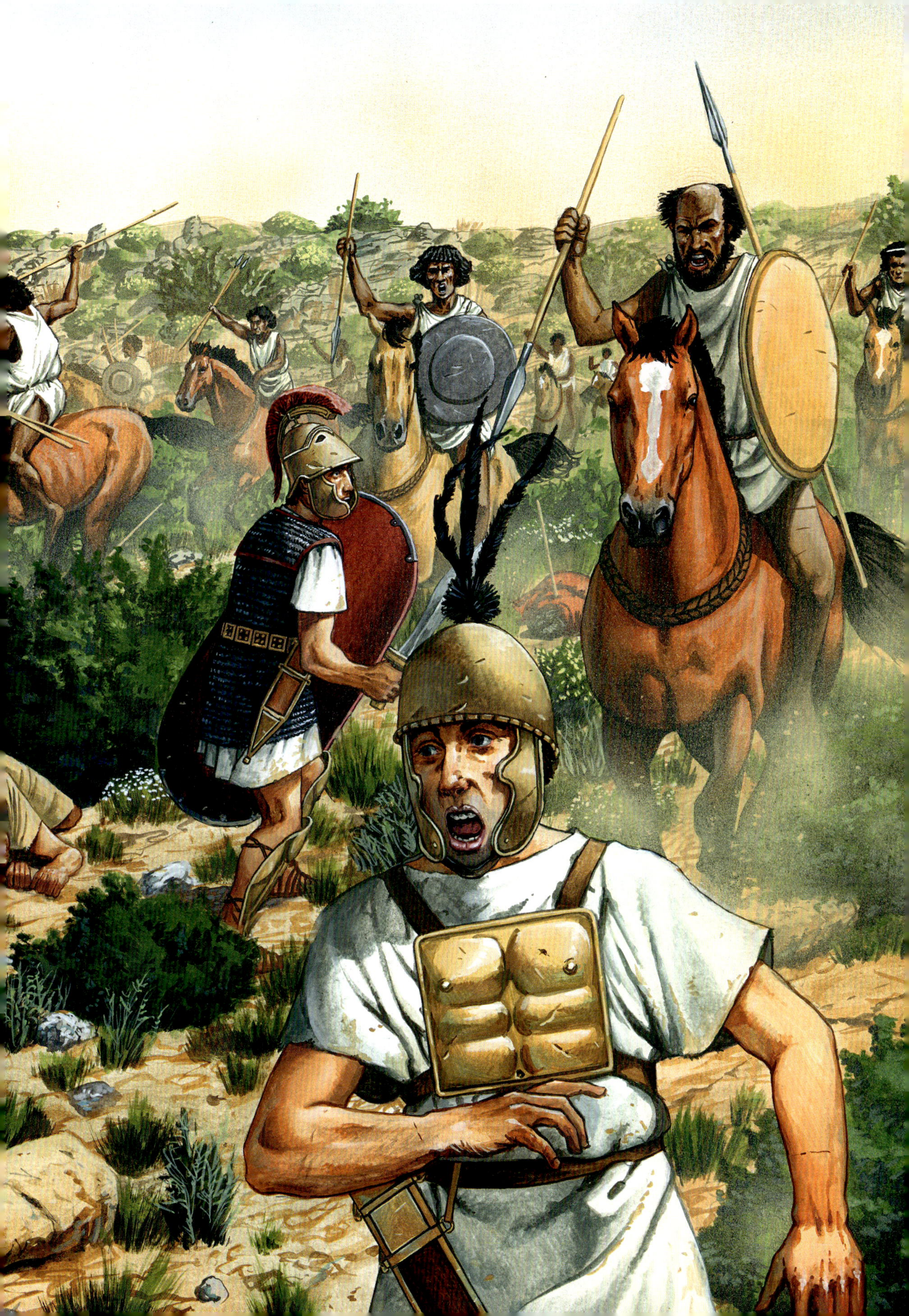

IGNOMINIOUS CAPITULATION OF AULUS POSTUMIUS ALBINUS, 110 BC (PP.50–51)

Having lifted his siege of Suthul, Aulus Postumius Albinus followed Jugurtha into increasingly distant parts of the kingdom. Once the Roman army was dangerously isolated, the king sprang his trap. Surrounding the Roman marching camp in the dead of night, he gave the prearranged signal for those he had previously bribed to make their move. One *cohors* of Ligures and two *turmae* of Thracians obliged. But the serious blow came when the chief centurion of *legio* III opened the gate he had been appointed to guard, allowing the Numidians to enter the camp. The Roman army collapsed into chaos and the survivors fled to a nearby hill, which turned out to be waterless, as the intruders busied themselves with plundering the camp.

The fog of war can be literal: for the shattered survivors on the following morning, it was clouds of dust thrown by thousands of horses' hooves **(1)**. True to form the Numidians swirled like smoke around the men on the hill, shouting and yelling and avoiding contact **(2)**. To the static observer, they are constantly turning, twisting and disappearing into their own dust, only to reappear again almost immediately at a different place. Even on the apparent safety of higher ground, the Romans began to learn the fear of encirclement – that cruel illness that afflicts the hearts, minds and legs of soldiers regardless of rank. The fact remains that men, however fleet of foot, cannot outrun horses: the words 'Every man for himself!' then sound like the height of wisdom **(3)**. As we witness in this reconstruction, what finally remained of Postumius Albinus' army was to struggle for its very existence. Despite the efforts of a few valiant men – a military tribune attempts to rally those around him **(4)**, a *triarius* chooses to stand and fight **(5)** – the outcome will be swift and grievous: defeat and degradation.

face death, the structures of military life become irrelevant. At the same time, creating certainty and fostering commitment are paramount because when the good commander exudes confidence and his commands and orders are clear and simple, when doubts have no chance to arise, the men will be confident and assured in their actions. Enthusiastic, unquestioned commitment will dispel doubt, carry men through battle and rob the enemy of his spirit, so causing fear, consternation and confusion in his ranks. Orders must never be issued lightly, nor should they be rescinded; otherwise, they lose their power and impact.

The fearsomeness of a commander in the midst of a campaign depends on the acceptance and execution of his orders and this execution depends on the fear, respect and willing allegiance of the men. Quite naturally, their respect is hard to win and could be snatched away in a single moment of cowardice or indecision. 'You should know that while success wins for commanders the goodwill of their men,' the Caesarian *legatus* Scribonius Curio explains to his war council, 'failure earns their hatred' (Caes. *B civ.* 2.31.6). Clearly, the most extensive efforts must be taken to preserve this interrelationship because once a crack such as doubt appears, the collapse of authority is

Marble votive stele (Teteven, Historical Museum) with bas-relief of the Thracian deity Heros in the guise of a javelin-armed Thracian horseman with a hound hunting a wild boar, 3rd century BC. Though he is bearing a round shield, Thracians remained unshielded until sometime in the 3rd century BC (cavalry shields first appear in Greece and Anatolia with the arrival of the Celts in 275 BC). In 168 BC, after the Third Macedonian War, Thrace became tributary to Rome. Thereafter, Thracian horsemen were recruited to serve in the Roman army as auxiliaries; a number of Thracians deserted during the Jugurthine War. (Spiritia, CC BY-SA 3.0 https://creativecommons.org/licenses/by-sa/3.0, via Wikimedia Commons)

imminent. Paradoxically, a man is not born a commander. He must become one through experience.

On his arrival in the province of Africa in the summer of 109 BC, Metellus had to knock the army he had inherited into proper shape. The soldiers were in poor condition after the command of the Postumii Albini, who had allowed the army to rot and decay (*B Iug.* 44.1). The soldiers had abandoned military routine to spend weeks in ill-disciplined idleness, not bothering fortifying or laying out their camp as per regulations, and shifting it only when forced to by lack of locally available forage or because the stench of their own waste became unbearable. Soldiers and camp followers raided and plundered at will.

Sallust represents Metellus as a man of energy and dispatch (*B Iug.* 43.2); he says specifically (B Iug. 45.3) that he soon had the army under control; that when it invaded Numidia it was alert and full of fight (*B Iug.* 46.5). Without a doubt, Metellus' response was a traditional one, namely to put the men back under the tight, all-embracing military discipline that the Roman Army was famed for. According to Eutropios, '[Metellus] brought the army, which had been ruined by previous generals, back to Roman discipline with great strictness and regulation but without being cruel' (Eutr. 4.27.2). Sellers, sutlers, slaves and other unscrupulous parasites were expelled, and soldiers forbidden to buy food. They had been in the habit of selling their rations of grain to purchase ready-baked civilian bread rather than eating the coarse camp bread they had to prepare

Citadel of Vaga (Béja, Tunisia), built during the reign of Justinianus I (AD 527–565) following the restoration of Africa as an imperial province in AD 533. When Jugurtha received the eastern half of the kingdom, Vaga was to serve as his capital. Apart from the battle by the Muthul, Metellus' campaigns centred around the border between the province of Africa and the kingdom of Numidia, specifically the towns of Vaga, Zama and Thala. (Pradigue, CC BY-SA 3.0 https://creativecommons.org/licenses/by-sa/3.0, via Wikimedia Commons)

and cook themselves. He also forbade 'the soldiers to use meat, except when roasted or boiled' (Frontin. 4.1.2). Metellus was clearly following the practice of slashing the 'tooth-to-tail' ratio introduced by Scipio Aemilianus at Numantia. He had ordered that meat was to be cooked either by roasting or boiling it, thereby reducing the number of cooking utensils to the standard three: a spit, *veru*, for roasting; a cooking pot, *trulleus*, for boiling; a mess tin, *patera*, for eating (App. *Iber.* 14 §85, cf. Frontin. 4.1.1, Polyain. 8.16.2). Ordinary ranks were barred from keeping their own servants or pack animals. Metellus ordered gruelling daily drills to reintroduce the men swiftly to the intricacies of military life, as well as to improve battle skill and endurance. From now on, the army broke camp every morning, and marched fully equipped to a new position where it constructed a marching camp as if in hostile territory. 'By these methods he was able to prevent breaches of discipline, and without having to inflict many punishments he soon restored the army's morale' (*B Iug.* 45.6).

Clearly no martinet, Metellus understood that when a commander leads his soldiers into battle, they must follow without hesitation. He worked hard to earn this loyalty by knowing and caring for his men. He is what we would call a good commander. With a natural inquisitiveness about how people perform, the good commander will connect to his soldiers in an intimate and personal way. Loyalty above all is based on appreciation. It develops when people appreciate what they are involved in and when appreciation is expressed for them. The good commander earns the loyalty of the soldiers by first genuinely expressing loyalty to them in even the smallest gestures. He does not miss the opportunity to win someone's trust and never gives up on anyone. In this way he creates a unified entity where before was an assembly of individuals and gains a fighting army that follows him through extreme conditions and conflict. Metellus was of this stamp.

Metellus' first campaign

Having knocked the army into shape, Metellus entered Numidia and seized Vaga (Béja, Tunisia). Jugurtha, meanwhile, was gathering strength while retreating. He employed his old devices by offering bribes to Metellus, if only he would grant peace. The intention of course was to beguile him into a sense of security and weaken him to the point where he could be easily defeated. But the king was now faced by an adversary he could not buy.

Marching south-westwards, crossing the Bagradas valley and the mountains beyond, Metellus soon had to fight a pitched battle, which after grievous hazards ended to the advantage of the Romans (*B Iug.* 48.3–53.8). The site of this confused whirling fight was close to the Muthul River, the principal right bank tributary of the Bagradas (Medjerda) River, not far to the north of Sicca (El Kef, Tunisia), a town that was to voluntarily come over to Metellus soon after (*B Iug.* 56.3).

Establishing a small detachment in Vaga to guard a supply dump he had established there and to protect its resident Italians, Metellus then pulled out. In the meantime, Jugurtha assembled his forces; horsemen, tribal levies and war elephants. The latter, 44 in number, along with part of the infantry, he placed under his chief lieutenant Bomilcar. He then got his men ahead of the Roman column-of-march and decided to fight among the rocky barren hills near the Muthul River. The king wanted the whole force of Metellus trapped. Having selected a position that would benefit him a wide field of view, he

The vast plain, formed by the Wādī Mallāq, near El Kef (ancient Sicca), Tunisia. It was this sort of terrain that was ideal for the highly mobile warfare that the Numidians so favoured. In a land of vast open spaces, the intruding Romans, who were mainly concerned with close-order infantry fighting, faced an enemy well acquainted with the country and enormously superior in guerrilla tactics. This was not the kind warfare envisaged in the training manuals of the Roman Army. (Rawene Sboui, CC BY-SA 4.0 https://creativecommons.org/licenses/by-sa/4.0, via Wikimedia Commons)

placed his men in a thin line along the top of a mountain spur overlooking the route he knew the Roman column-of-march would pass along. The spur was 'clothed with wild olive, myrtles, and other varieties of trees that grow from a dry and sandy soil' (*B Iug.* 48.3). He hid his men as best he could among the spur's low scrub vegetation and dead ground and concealed his banners and flags so as not to advertise his whereabouts. He then waited for the moment of ambush.

Descending from a mountain, the Roman column was slowly uncoiling and heading towards the Muthul when Metellus spotted to his right the ambush against the browns, greys and greens of the muted landscape. He immediately halted the column and re-formed in line-of-battle facing to the right of his previous direction: what had been his vanguard became his left flank; his rearguard became his right flank.

Now in battle formation – presumably the usual *triplex acies* – the Romans were facing the nearby scrub-covered spur, which was now bristling with war-caparisoned Numidians. Metellus distributed archers and slingers between the maniples. All his cavalry were stationed on the wings.

Jugurtha did not attack at once. Possibly he had to rethink his tactics and reorder his men accordingly. Metellus, concerned that his men were worn down by thirst and fatigue, sent one of his *legati*, Publius Rutilius Rufus, with a body of horse and a number of allied *cohortes* in fighting order (*B Iug.* 50.1) down into the riverine plain to establish a marching camp beside the Muthul. As this small detachment, presumably from *ala sinistra*, passed below the Numidians, Bomilcar proceeded after it with his infantry and elephants.

Then with quiet steadiness, the main Roman body faced left and became a column (*agmen*) once more. With Metellus and 'cavalry of the left wing' (*B Iug.* 50.2) acting as vanguard, and his other *legatus*, Caius Marius, delegated to command the infantry, the column descended slowly but surely into the riverine plain. As the tail end of the column reached level ground – presumably the rearguard consisting of the cavalry of the right wing – Jugurtha sent some 2,000 men to occupy the route through which the enemy had passed with the intention of trapping them in the plain, which was, excluding the herders subsisting along the Muthul, uninhabited owing to its aridity. The rest of the king's command then shadowed the Romans below.

The situation around Metellus developed quickly. The Numidian shadowing movement transformed into an all-out attack. Jugurtha began to assault the column's flanks with his nimble horsemen, who dashed hither and thither casting their javelins. When pursued, they simply melted away,

Wādī Mallāq, Tunisia, Sallust's Muthul, a tributary of the Medjerda (Bagradas) river. Sallust's description of the battle in 109 BC near the Muthul (*B Iug.* 48.3–53.8) contains an exceptional amount of topographical and tactical detail. He was clearly following an eyewitness account of Rutilius Rufus, one of Metellus' *legati*. (Oussemos, CC BY-SA 3.0 https://creativecommons.org/licenses/by-sa/3.0, via Wikimedia Commons)

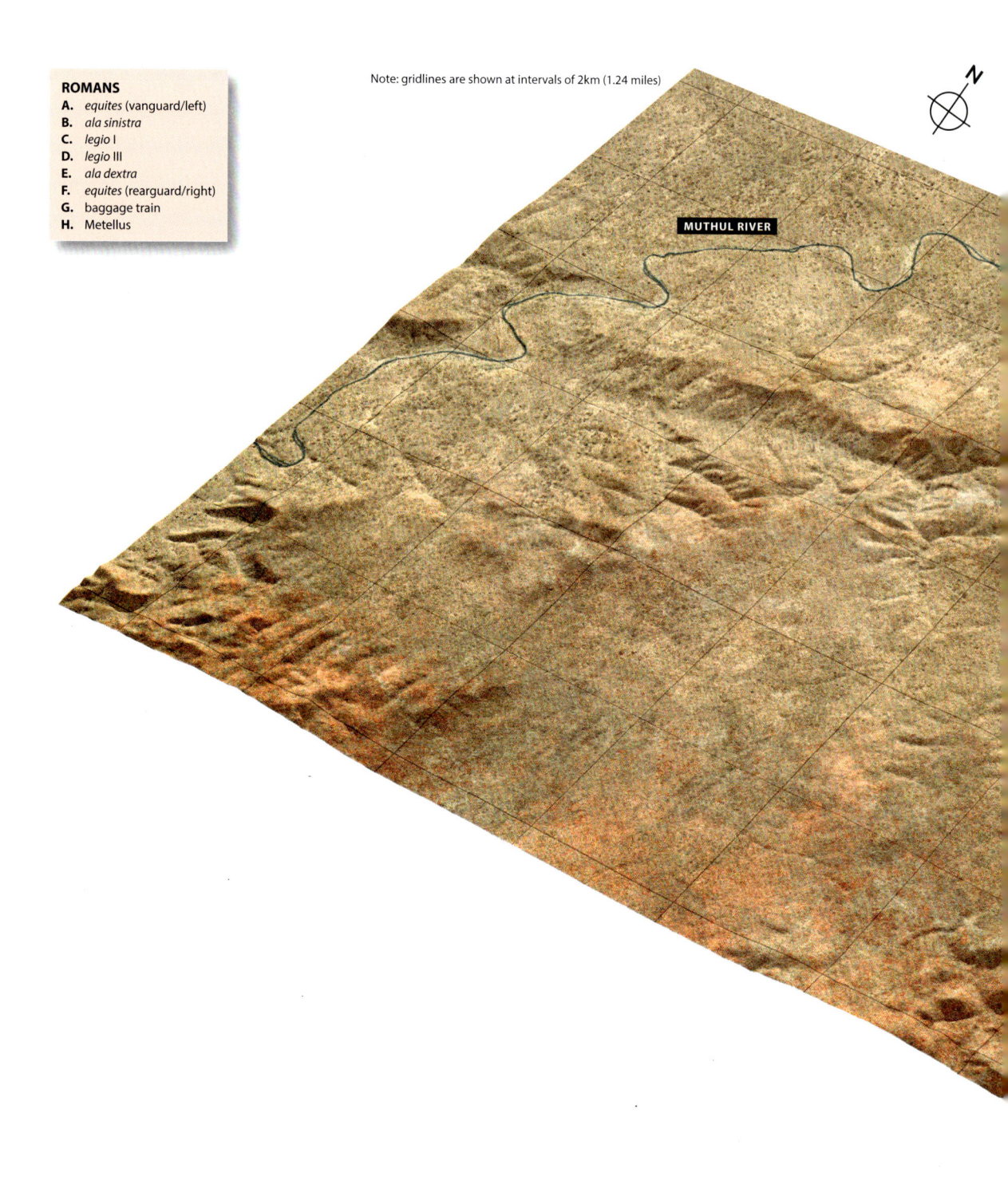

ROMANS
A. *equites* (vanguard/left)
B. *ala sinistra*
C. *legio* I
D. *legio* III
E. *ala dextra*
F. *equites* (rearguard/right)
G. baggage train
H. Metellus

Note: gridlines are shown at intervals of 2km (1.24 miles)

MUTHUL RIVER

▼ **EVENTS**

1. Jugurtha positions his Numidians on a mountain spur overlooking the descent into a riverine plain where they would be in clear view of the advancing Roman column of route. Bomilcar, commanding the elephants and a detachment of foot, is stationed further down the spur.

2. The long Roman column of route winds its way down the mountainside heading for the plain and the Muthul River.

3. Having spotted the Numidian ambush to his right, Metellus orders the column to halt and for each man to turn to his right, so forming a *triplex acies* facing the enemy. The baggage train, originally stationed between the *equites* forming the rearguard and *ala dextra* to its front, takes a position to the rear of the battleline.

THE MUTHUL 109 BC: OPENING MOVES

When it came to facing Metellus, there were two ways in which Jugurtha could handle it. He might choose a strong position across his line-of-march, thus challenging him to a pitched battle. Obviously, in such a scenario he would take unnecessary casualties. But another plan was open to Jugurtha, one more suited to the Numidian style of warfare. He could assail the consul's army where it was stretched out in a long column of route at a location lacking in sufficient elbow room. It was in a tight spot that an army on the march could be overwhelmed. However, to do so would take patience, discipline and good timing.

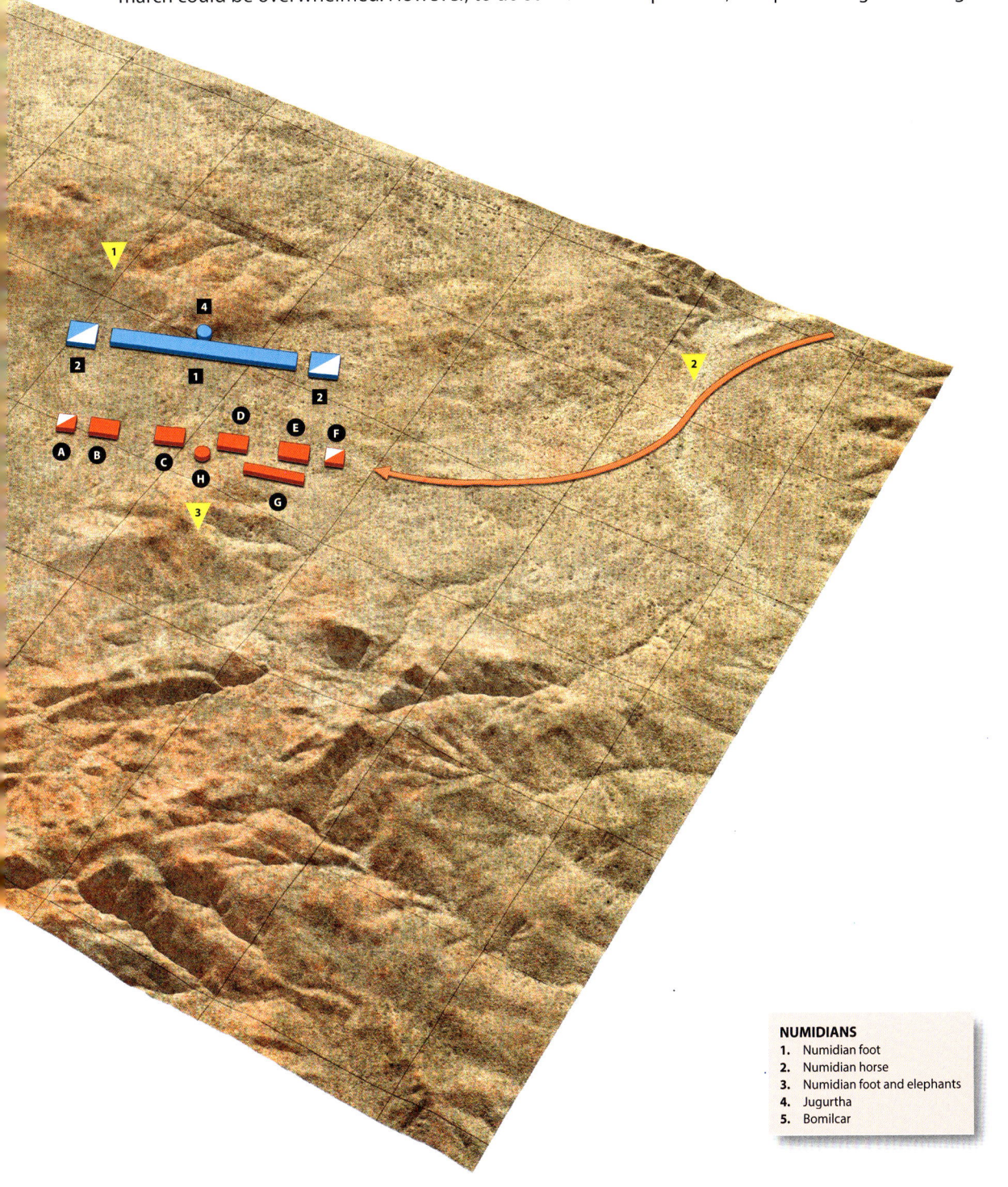

NUMIDIANS
1. Numidian foot
2. Numidian horse
3. Numidian foot and elephants
4. Jugurtha
5. Bomilcar

African forest elephant, Dzanga Bai, Central African Republic. The African forest elephant is 2.15–2.45m tall at the shoulder, shorter in stature than the Indian elephant, and much smaller than the great bush elephant of present-day Central and West Africa. Other differences between the species include the African's more strongly segmented trunk, ending in two 'fingers' rather than one, and the line of its back is concave, whereas the Indian's is convex. The forest elephant also has ears with enormous flaps and rounded lobes, and little straight tusks. The forest elephant was a breed that was still native in parts of Africa in great numbers, including on the coast of Mauretania. (Joris Komen, CC BY-SA 2.0 https://creativecommons.org/licenses/by-sa/2.0, via Wikimedia Commons)

fleeing in all directions and trying to cut off any isolated *equites* they could find. Sallust says that these shoot-and-scoot assaults disordered all the ranks (*B Iug*. 51.1), which suggests the column was caught off-guard before it could properly deploy into battle formation. Even so, there was a good deal of hot fighting at close quarters, and a successful charge by 'four legionary cohorts' (*B Iug*. 51.3)[8] towards a number of fatigued Numidians who had pulled back upon higher ground put an end to the engagement in this quarter. Most of these Numidians slipped silently away into the surrounding scrub, leaving windrows of corpses and badly wounded with the Romans.

In the meantime, Metellus and Jugurtha both exerted themselves in rallying and exhorting their respective forces. As Sallust makes clear, 'Metellus had valiant soldiers but an unfavourable position, while Jugurtha had favourable circumstances in all else except his soldiers' (*B Iug*. 52.2). In short: a final, desperate charge up the spur by the Romans clinched the day.

Elsewhere, a separate battle took place near the Muthul. Rutilius Rufus and his detachment, having found a suitable site, had marked out a marching camp and the soldiers begun to entrench. At this point a great cloud of dust appeared before them. They guessed at first that it was merely dust that had been carried up by the wind – the plain was broken country covered with prickly, unpleasant scrub – and it was difficult to see that it was really a sign

---

[8] Legionary cohorts, as opposed to those of the Italian *socii* (*B Iug*. 38.6, 46.7, 50.1), are referred to once more by Sallust (100.4), this time during Marius' second campaign. After this war the maniple as a tactical formation is not heard of again.

of the approaching Numidian detachment under Bomilcar. There was no sense of urgency yet. The soldiers continued with their labour. But when they saw the dust cloud was not dispersing but getting nearer, they grabbed their arms and, pouncing upon the advancing Numidians, the rest was quickly over. To return to Sallust's account, 'The Numidians stood their ground only so long as they looked for help from the elephants; after they saw that the beasts had become entangled in the branches of the trees and were thus thrown into disarray and surrounded, they took to flight' (*B Iug.* 53.3).

Having taken to their heels, the victors slaughtered all but four of the elephants. The sudden fall of night meant that the *equites* of the divided Roman force met in the dark. Luckily, they recognized each other, which thus enabled the weary column to reach the camp. All told, Metellus had just managed to win a confused, hard-fought and expensive victory in the dusty and oppressive heat of Numidia.

Apart from the 44 elephants (*B Iug.* 53.4), Sallust gives no figures for either side. In fact, the historian eschews any estimate of numbers (along with chronology) in the Jugurthine War, even on the Roman side. Metellus presumably had a standard consular army of two Roman *legiones* – possibly *legiones* I and III (see *B Iug.* 38.6) – and two Latin/Italian *alae*, say some 20,000 men. It may have been smaller – he must have left troops to garrison various towns, such as Vaga, and also to protect the province of Africa, but then he had brought some additional manpower with him when he took up his command, so 20,000 men seems a good guess. As for Jugurtha, it is impossible to say. In the aftermath of the battle, Metellus spent four days by the Muthul, allowing his men to rest and the wounded to recover.

Jugurtha got clean away. After this setback, according to Frontinus (2.1.13), the king always began engagements in the evening so that his men could take advantage of darkness to get away if they were defeated. As for Metellus, wary of heavy losses in pitched battles against an unencumbered and highly mobile enemy, he would settle down to a piecemeal conquest. Even so, Metellus would fail to bring the war to a conclusion – the problem was physically capturing Jugurtha. Metellus, therefore, resorted to bribery coupled with a policy of reducing the urban communities in Numidia so as to deprive Jugurtha logistically. Marius was to employ the same strategy against Jugurtha, so we should be wary of any criticism of Metellus' conduct in Numidia. That all said, there was a senatorial tradition glorifying Metellus, asserting that he had broken the back of Jugurtha's resistance when for reasons of (unjust) home politics he was replaced by Marius (Liv. *Per.* 65, Vell. 2.11.2, Flor. 1.36.10–12, Eutr. 4.27.2).

With the geography of Numidia, Sallust, erstwhile Caesarian governor of Africa Nova – hence his brief ethnographic sketch of the peoples dwelling in the coastal regions of northern Africa (*B Iug.* 17.1–19.8) – is economical, specifying only three rivers (Muthul, Tanais, Muluccha) and seven settlements (Vaga, Sicca, Zama, Cirta, Thala, Capsa, Lares) in the theatre of operations covered by the marches and battles of Metellus and Marius. So, all we can learn from Sallust's narrative about the Muthul is that it flowed in a northerly direction (*B Iug.* 48.3), that it was in the eastern part of Numidia (op. cit.), and that Metellus had recently passed near Vaga and was probably marching southward.

We can assume this was all for brevity and not wishing to overburden the narration, but in truth, accuracy to him was of small importance compared

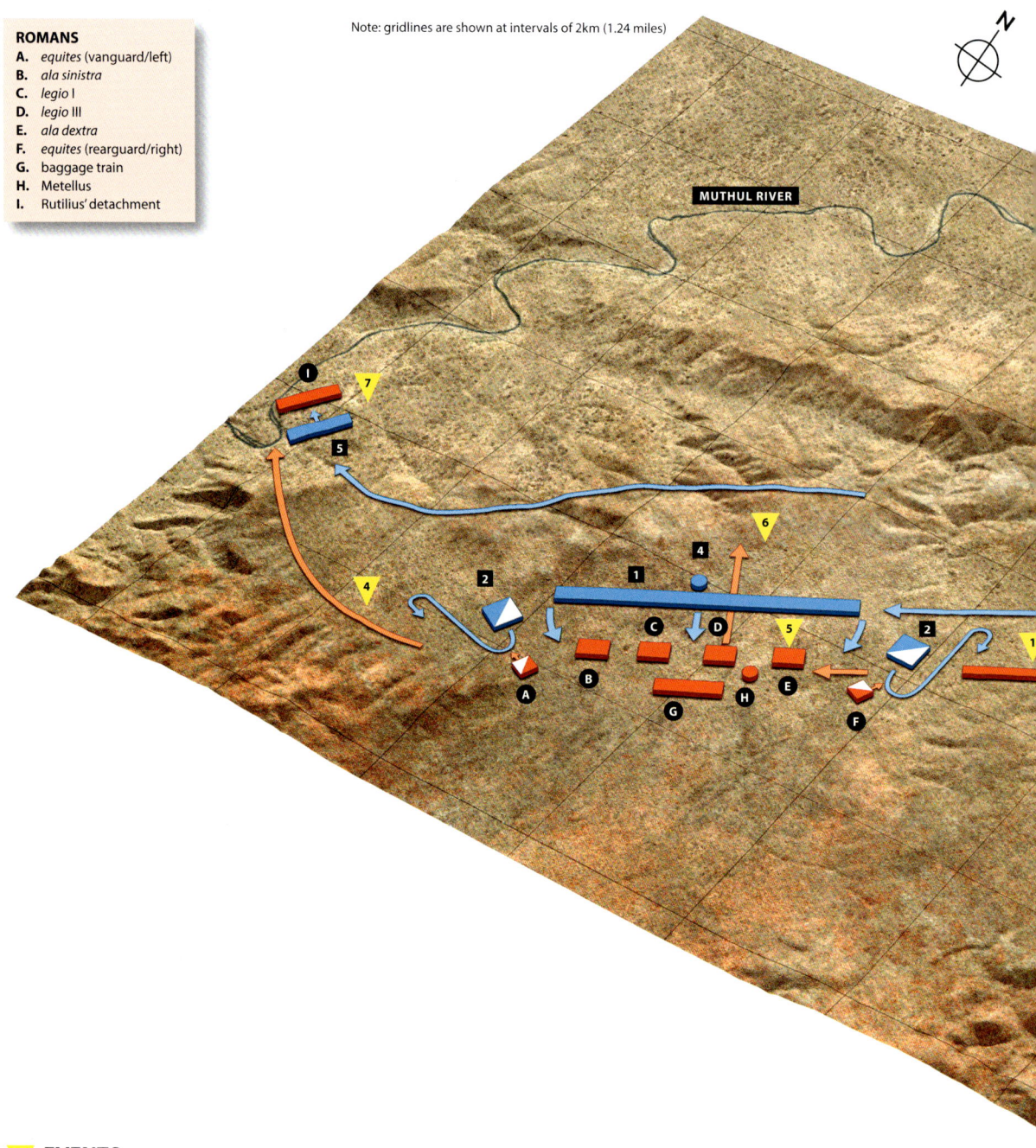

ROMANS
A. *equites* (vanguard/left)
B. *ala sinistra*
C. *legio* I
D. *legio* III
E. *ala dextra*
F. *equites* (rearguard/right)
G. baggage train
H. Metellus
I. Rutilius' detachment

Note: gridlines are shown at intervals of 2km (1.24 miles)

MUTHUL RIVER

▼ EVENTS

1. His ambush having failed, Jugurtha initially remains inactive: Metellus orders each man to turn to his left, so re-forming the column of route. Metellus leads the column with the *equites* forming the vanguard.

2. The Romans having recommenced their descent towards the riverine plain, Jugurtha follows. Nonetheless, the king continues to exploit the topography of the area by keeping his army on the spur.

3. To prevent any retreat by that route, a Numidian detachment takes up a position at the eastern entrance to the plain, the Roman column of route having already passed by.

4. Rutilius Rufus, leading a body of horse and a number of Latin/Italian *cohortes* from *ala sinistra*, is ordered to head for the Muthul in order to establish an overnight marching camp; Bomilcar, leading his Numidian foot and elephants, shadows him along the spur.

5. The Numidians suddenly attack and the Roman column attempts to form a triple line-of-battle facing the spur: Numidians and Romans become mingled in a confused fight. Metellus gradually unites his soldiers and reconstitutes the battleline; Jugurtha likewise rallies his men and renews the struggle.

6. Four *cohortes* from *legio* III mount a charge up the spur, clearing the Numidians in this quarter. A final, desperate charge up the spur by the remaining Romans clinches the day.

7. In the meantime, Rutilius Rufus and Bomilcar engage beside the Muthul: with the elephants compromised by the rough terrain, Rutilius Rufus gains a victory.

THE MUTHUL 109 BC: CRISIS OF BATTLE

Surprise and ambush of course are linked together; an ambush after all depends on surprise being achieved. Surprise is twofold, namely, surprise brought about by doing something that the enemy does not expect (moral surprise), and surprise brought about by doing something that the enemy cannot counter (material surprise). In both cases, Jugurtha's ambush failed. All the same, being on higher ground offered significant advantages to the Numidians, including the psychological advantage of looking down on its enemy, and the practical one of a panoramic view.

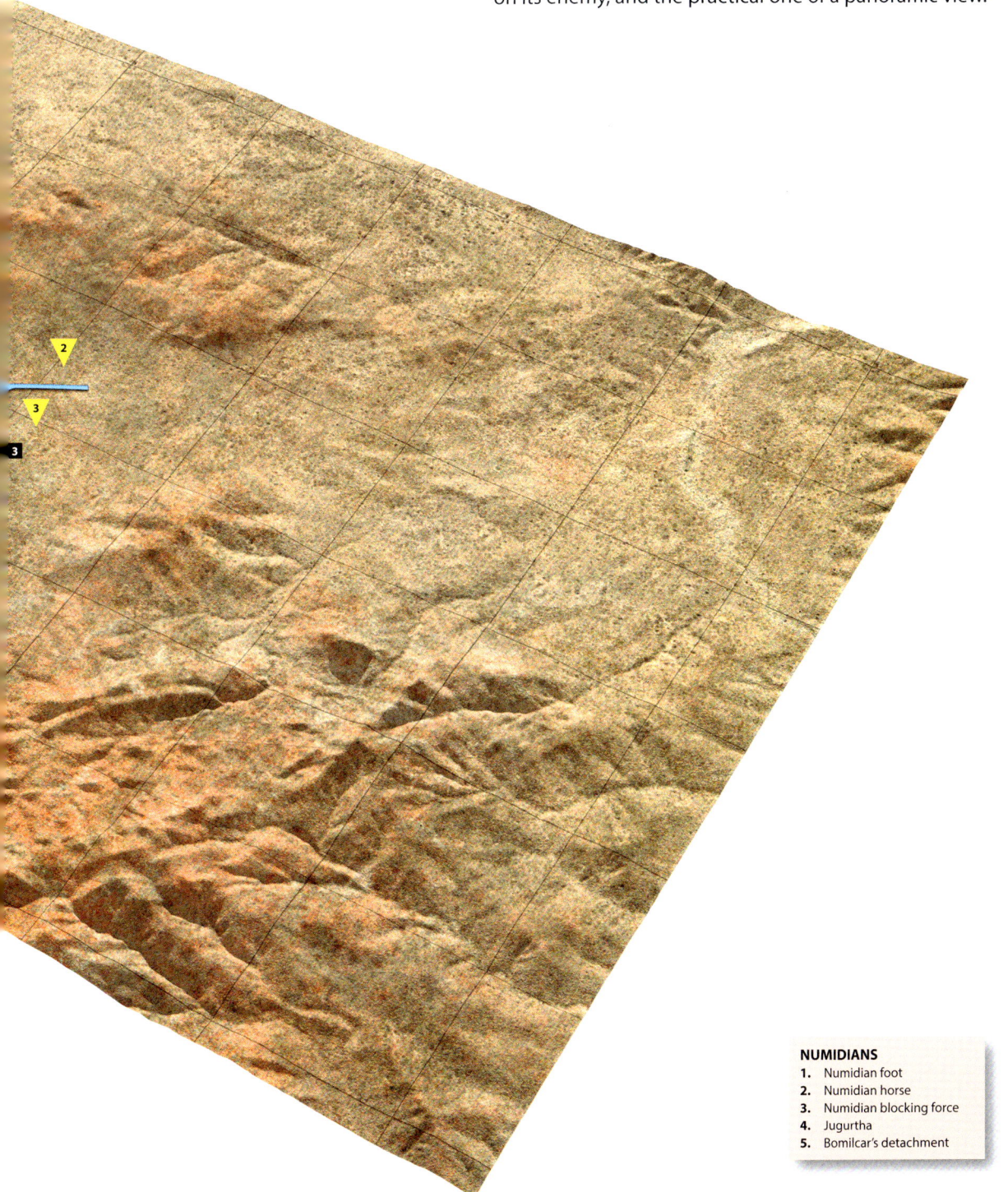

NUMIDIANS
1. Numidian foot
2. Numidian horse
3. Numidian blocking force
4. Jugurtha
5. Bomilcar's detachment

Military reenactors equipped and armed as Polybian legionaries, Gergovie plateau, Les Arverniales, 2012. From left to right, two *velites*, a dismounted *eques* in a Boiotian helmet, five legionaries and a *veles*. (Elliott Sadourny, CC BY-SA 3.0 https://creativecommons.org/licenses/by-sa/3.0, via Wikimedia Commons)

with the chance of drawing a moral lesson. Sallust's account of the Muthul, however, is the one true exception. The excellent narration (*B Iug.* 48.3–53.8) of this crucial battle betrays considerable knowledge of Rutilius Rufus' memoirs. Rutilius Rufus was very much interested in the science of warfare, and was to gain a well-deserved reputation as a military theorist and author, though sadly for us these memoirs, which were composed in Greek, have been extinguished by the malevolence of time.

It was Rutilius Rufus, as one of the consuls of 105 BC, who was to introduce the methods of the gladiatorial schools so as 'to train his legionaries in a more skilful technique of weaponry, both in attack and in defence' (Val. Max. 2.3.2). The following year, while he was busy making preparations for the war against the Cimbri and the Teutones, Marius was so impressed by the legionaries trained by Rutilius Rufus that he preferred them to his own, choosing 'the army of Rutilius, though it was the smaller of the two, because he thought it was the better trained' (Frontin. 4.2.2). Reading between the lines, it does suggest that the Numidian army of Marius was either blown or full of unpromising recruits.

After the bruising fight at the Muthul, Metellus 'decided that he must conduct the campaign not by pitched battles and in set formation but in another fashion' (*B Iug.* 54.5): he marched into the richest part of Numidia, 'laid waste the fields, captured and burned many strongholds and towns [*multa castella et oppida*] carelessly fortified or garrisoned, ordered adults to be killed and all else to be his soldiers' booty' (*B Iug.* 54.6).

Having slashed and burned swathes of Numidia, leaving ruined settlements behind him to mark his track, the final act of Metellus' first campaign was a vain attempt to capture Zama (later Zama Regia). Jugurtha, having cobbled together another army, offered resistance and a fierce battle ensued in the vicinity of the town (*B Iug.* 56.1–60.8). The king had strengthened the garrison there with a sprinkling of deserters from the Roman army, desperadoes who dared not fail in their task to doggedly defend the town in the awareness of the terrible punishment meted out to those who forsook Rome. After the failure of two days of assaults, and two determined attacks on his camp, Metellus abandoned the siege and retreated. Leaving garrisons in those towns that had come under his control, Metellus took up winter quarters in the province of Africa, but close to its border with Numidia (*B Iug.* 61.2), possibly at Tisidium (Crich-El-Oued, Tunisia) on the Bagradas. Metellus summoned Jugurtha to come there (*B Iug.* 62.8).

The winter witnessed the sudden loss (through treachery) and swift recapture (through trickery) of Vaga. Metellus was deeply grieved by the Vaga plot and exacted his revenge upon the town by luring the inhabitants out of the walls, with his army screened by Numidian horsemen (*B Iug.* 69.1) – we hear of many Numidians on the Roman side at various times. A sudden signal and the slaughter of the inhabitants began (*B Iug.* 69.2). So retribution was obtained. But Metellus' wrath was not to end there. Thracian and Ligurum deserters were among the survivors, '[Metellus] cut off the hands of some, and others he buried in the earth up to their stomachs, and after transfixing them with arrows and darts set fire to them while they were still alive' (App. *Num.* fr. 3). Even by Roman standards, this was a nasty, brutish thing. The war in Africa was turning out to be a spiteful one and would only get bloodier from here.

While encamped in winter quarters, Metellus intrigued with Jugurtha's confident Bomilcar, who had managed to escape the misadventure at the Muthul. This was the same Bomilcar who had been implicated years before in the murder of Massiva in Rome. Regardless, Bomilcar unsuccessfully tried to persuade Jugurtha to surrender to Metellus (*B Iug.* 62.1–4). Shortly, Bomilcar was duly executed when discovered in an assassination plot against his king (*B Iug.* 72.1). And the palace intrigues did not end there. On at least three occasions Metellus also bribed the envoys sent to him by Jugurtha.

The ruins of Roman Zama Regia. Originally Zama, the town's inhabitants – along with some Roman and Italian deserters – successfully resisted the siege conducted by Metellus at the end of his first campaign in 109 BC. Jugurtha, having conjured up yet another army, fought a pitched battle against Metellus nearby. (Astiosaurus, CC BY-SA 4.0 https://creativecommons.org/licenses/by-sa/4.0, via Wikimedia Commons)

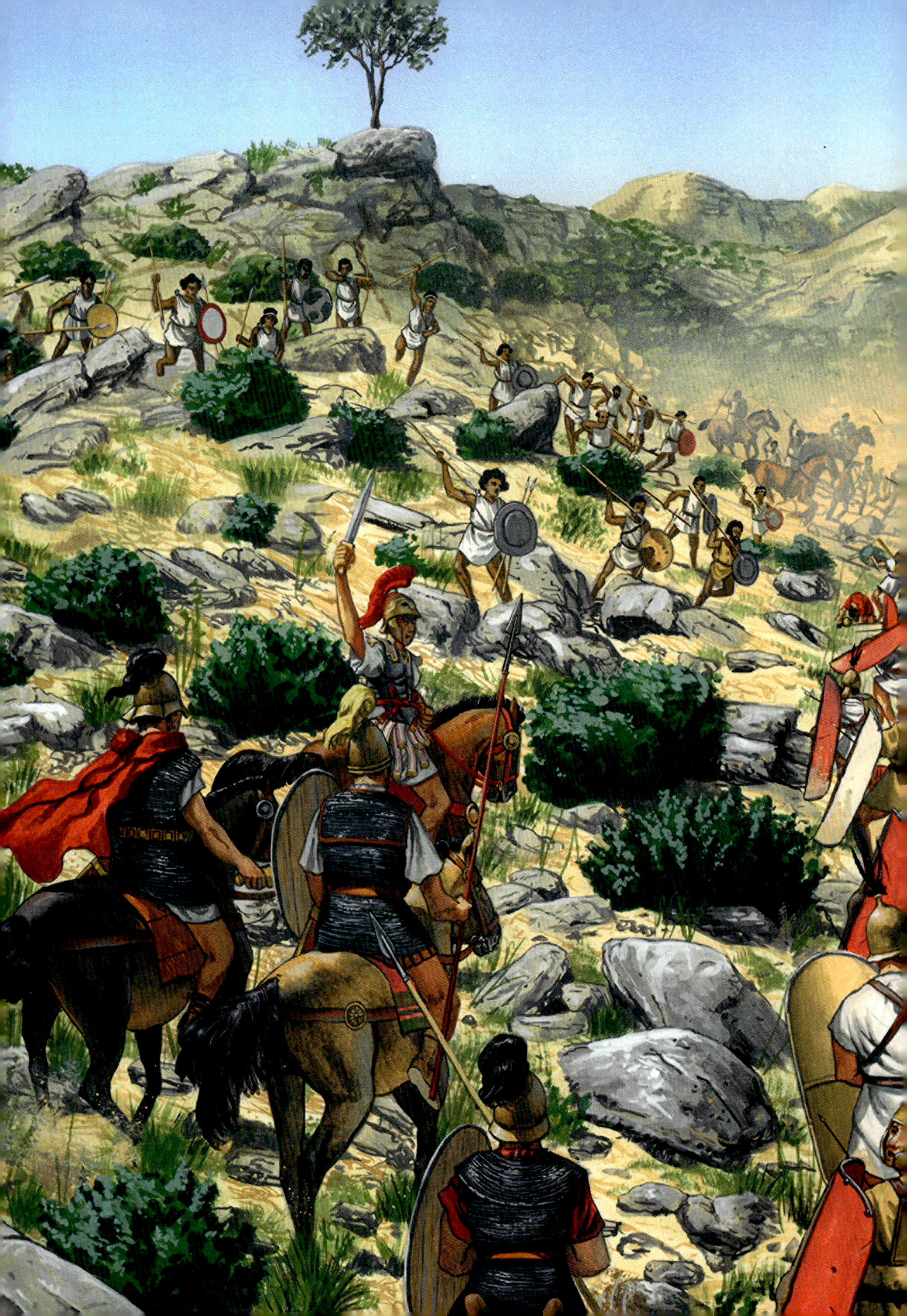

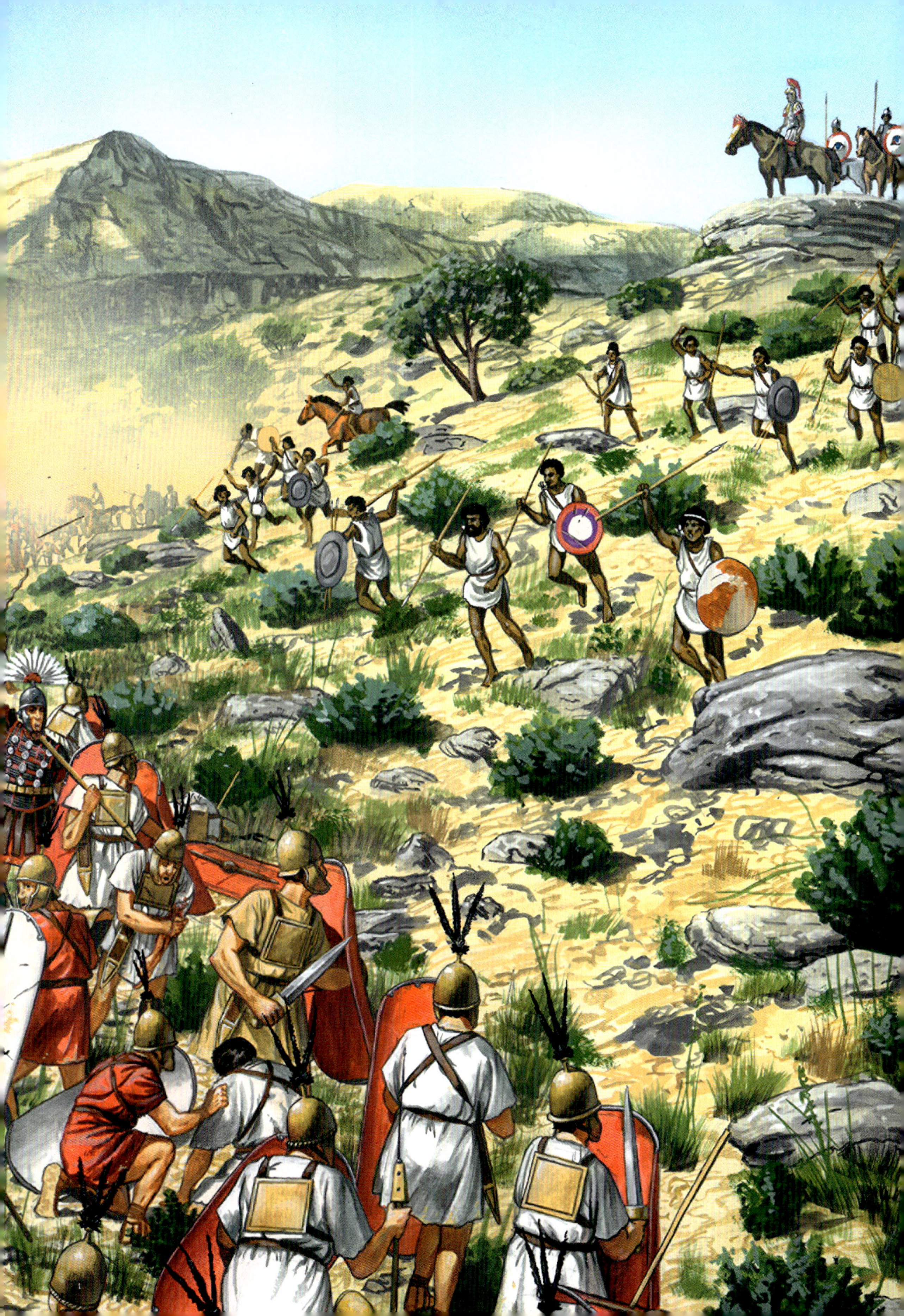

THE BATTLE OF THE MUTHUL, 109 BC (PP.66–67)

As any contemporary soldier knows, an ambush is a surprise attack, by a force lying in wait, upon a moving or temporarily halted enemy. It is usually a brief encounter and does not require the capture and holding of ground. Almost invariably the action will take place at close range. There are two types of ambush, namely deliberate (by design) and immediate (by an inspiration of the moment). The first type is planned and executed as an independent operation. Frequently it will be easier to achieve success with a small ambush rather than a large one. The second type is one set with a minimum of planning to anticipate imminent enemy action. The total success of its execution relies on the initiative and agility of the commander and the ability and discipline of his men. In both cases, as the commander cannot see the whole of his command, the need for maintaining concealment, and the absence of movement, noise and smell while in hiding, is an absolute must. Ultimately, a cleverly concealed ambush will not only achieve surprise but also catch the enemy when he is least expecting to be ambushed.

His deliberate ambush having failed, Jugurtha has resorted to engaging the Romans in battle. Battles are dangerous affairs and soldiers, even to this day, are heavily dependent on agility and foot speed for both their survival and aggressiveness. Yet the Roman soldier, like all soldiers before his day and after, was grossly overloaded with kit. Often, in the heaviest hours, when they were drowsily advancing under an alien sky and over an equally alien landscape weighed down by war gear, a great line of brown dust would suddenly arise on the horizon; a host of centaur-like Numidians with blistering hoof speed would appear, and out of a cloud a hail of javelins would rain down.

In this reconstruction, despite having spotted Jugurtha's ambush, Metellus' marching column has been badly compromised and his men are struggling to form a line-of-battle **(1)**. As Numidian warriors come barrelling down the spur headlong into the disordered Roman column **(2)**, Numidian horsemen are starting to menace its flanks **(3)**. Jugurtha, accompanied by his royal bodyguard, is to seen up on the high ground watching the battle unfold **(4)**.

Clearly, this was an attempt to put Jugurtha out of the way once and for all. It failed (*B Iug.* 70–72). Indeed, Metellus had opened his Numidian adventure with an attempt to ensnare or to liquidate Jugurtha, tampering with the king's envoys before he even took the field (*B Iug.* 46.4). He tried again after the occupation of Vaga (*B Iug.* 47.4). So, from the start Metellus was willing to employ the treachery and double-dealing of Jugurtha and, according to Frontinus (1.8.8), he even urged the envoys to deliver their master prisoner to him. For the same purpose, Metellus kept up a correspondence with them after they had departed until Jugurtha grew so suspicious of these men that he had them done away with.

Metellus' second campaign

Metellus' command in Numidia had been prorogued by a decree of the Senate (*B Iug.* 62.10), whereupon the *pro consule* took the field once again (*B Iug.* 73.1). There followed a battle in which Jugurtha was worsted. The king retired into the arid lands of his kingdom and took asylum at the desert town of Thala (Tunisia), where his children and much of his treasure were stashed. Undaunted, Metellus marched across the sun-parched wastes to the town and took it following a siege of 40 days. Jugurtha slipped away with his children and the bulk of his treasure and fled into the mountainous land of the Gaetulians. Metellus had slogged his army to Thala 'in the hope of ending the war' (*spe patrandi belli*: *B Iug.* 75.2). After a time, he induced Bocchus, the king of Mauretania, who happened to be Jugurtha's father-in-law, to intervene and lend a hand. Matters gathered apace, and the two kings appeared in force near Cirta, that finest of natural strongholds which had at some time come into Roman possession (*B Iug.* 81.2).

Negotiations followed and warfare lapsed (*B Iug.* 83.3). Metellus meanwhile had received news from Rome not only that Caius Marius, his one-time *legatus*, had been elected to the consulship – considered by the

General view of Thala. Nestling upon two desolate hills, Thala (elev. 1,017m) is the highest and coldest town in Tunisia. When Jugurtha ruled Numidia as one kingdom, he chose Thala, 'a large and wealthy town' (*B Iug.* 75.1), as his capital, functioning as the chief royal treasury. Metellus besieged it in the summer of 108 BC during his second campaign, surrounding the town with a ditch and palisade. Jugurtha, however, successfully slipped away with most of his treasure and his children under the cover of night. Metellus' capture of Thala, after a 40-day siege, was in itself a valuable achievement. (MnasriT, CC BY-SA 3.0 https://creativecommons.org/licenses/by-sa/3.0, via Wikimedia Commons)

likes of Metellus the close preserve of the *nobilitas* (*B Iug*. 63.6) – but that Numidia had been assigned to Marius too: 'Upset by this news more than was right or proper, he neither held back tears nor curbed his tongue; an outstanding man in other qualities, he was too soft in enduring stress' (*B Iug*. 82.2, cf. 45.1). To right-thinking men, it was outrageous if a *novus homo* got so far (*B Iug*. 63.7). Obviously, little did the horrified Metellus realize at the time that this consulship would prove to be the first of seven, more than any man, let alone a *novus homo*, had ever held before. What is even more startling is that five were to be held in consecutive years between 104 BC and 100 BC, while the seventh Marius seized in 86 BC, in the grim insanity of his final months, with armed force. This was to prove the last glint of the Marian sun.

Marius' political trajectory tells a sorry tale. Politically brazen, amoral and venal, the man from Arpinum was the interloper, the disruptor and, in many ways, his remarkable career was to provide a model for the warring warlords of the last decades of the Republic. For Sallust, the Jugurthine War does not end with Jugurtha (*B Iug*. 5.2), but morphs initially into the *Bellum Italicum* (91–88 BC), followed by the civil wars between Sulla and the Marians (88–82 BC), Caesar and the Pompeians (49–46 BC) and, most recently for Sallust, the Triumvirs and the Liberators (42 BC). In his apposite words, force was paving the way for 'bloodshed, exile, and other horrors of war' (*B Iug*. 3.2). The wars went on, and the Republic was crushed at Philippi.

Hitherto the campaigns of 109 BC and 108 BC had seen Metellus repeatedly compromise Jugurtha – he was to come home to immense and well-deserved popular acclaim and to rightly earn a triumph and the cognomen *Numidicus*

The northern slopes of Djebel Akouker (elev. 2,184m) in the Djurdjura, Algeria. The Djurdjura massif, a sub-range of the Tell Atlas, was known as Mons Ferratus (Iron Mountains) to the Romans. When Jugurtha took to the Tell Atlas, with its sharp peaks and saw-like ridges, the king was down but not out: he would skirmish with the Roman forces or fight them on his own terms. (Farid Ait Chaalal, CC BY-SA 4.0 https://creativecommons.org/licenses/by-sa/4.0, via Wikimedia Commons)

for his efforts (Vell. 2.11.2, Eutr. 4.27.6) – but had found it impossible to bring Jugurtha to heel: the king of the Numidians remained at large in the dusty, serpent-infested land, much of which was devoid of water. Metellus had learned to adapt his tactics to find and fight an elusive cunning foe, but there was to be no high noon showdown between the two. Jugurtha, who was sufficiently wise not to mass his tribal levies for a set-piece battle in open country, displayed extraordinary flexibility. Defeated at Thala, he melted into the semi-desert, whence he returned even stronger than ever. He would only skirmish with the Roman forces or fight them on his own terms, utilizing the tactics of surprise, feigned retreats and ambush. With the eye of a hawk and the stealth of a wolf, he had the kind of bravery – the most effective kind – that derived from playing only when one is assured of victory.

With their emphasis on fitness and fleetness, the Numidians had three societal diversions, and of Jugurtha it was said, '[H]e did not allow himself to be spoiled by luxury or idleness, but following the custom of that nation, he rode horses, hurled the javelin, contended with those of his same age in footraces, and although he surpassed them all in renown, he nevertheless enjoyed the affection of all' (*B Iug.* 6.1). Sallust may be thinking of the education of Persian nobles, as described by Herodotos – 'to ride, to use the bow, and to speak the truth' (1.136). Of prime importance for the Numidians, however, was the ability to ride and fight well. Worked on until they became proficient in both, such athletic pursuits undoubtedly steeled the Numidians for the style of war they preferred to pursue.

Jugurtha himself appears to have been singularly adapted for ruling his people. Yet like many dynamic rulers, he was a heady blend of contradictions, at once conscientious and cutthroat, capricious and careful, cruel and compassionate. This may be a case of history being construed by the victors. Yet Jugurtha, if not Sallust's favourite sinister villain in the story, does come across as the stuff of a dark fable. Jugurtha knew that martial arts were not the only means to victory in war: the dark arts of murder, deception and bribery were important too.

Sallust saw that the constant failure to overcome the Numidian king was in part due to Roman incompetence, with a deeper reason down to the corruption of the Roman *nobilitas*. Of those who doubted the danger of Jugurtha, Sallust saw that their attitude could only be accounted for by the sort of toleration a man extends to his pet wolf who, living in the house like a dog, only eats his neighbours' sheep and occasionally their children too. With the benefit of 20/20 hindsight, it is easy to affirm that Jugurtha was of such a nature.

It is the fancy of the human psyche to exalt chosen villains above their infamy, and quite often we are on the side of the roguish underdog. On balance, for the reader of *Bellum Iugurthinum* there is a vicarious thrill in championing Sallust's beleaguered anti-hero, the no-holds-barred opportunist who tries but fails to overcome an overwhelming external threat.

MARIUS TAKES COMMAND

Despite being bitter, Metellus accepted the change in command in 107 BC. According to Velleius Paterculus, who was no fan of a *novus homo* he thought a rustic with a rough and uncouth personality who was a malevolence in peacetime, possessed of insatiable ambition, without self-control and perpetually unstable: '[Marius] had the chief command of the war placed in his own hands, although the war had already been practically ended by Metellus, who had twice defeated Jugurtha in battle' (Vell. 2.11.2).

According to this version of events (also Flor. 1.36.11–13, Eutr. 4.27.2–3), Metellus did most of the heavy lifting. True, Marius did not bring with him any fresh ideas on how to fight or even win a war conducted in country favouring the enemy, he simply continued his predecessor's methods, perhaps on a larger scale and certainly over a wider area. But he did, on the other hand, realize that the anti-insurgent war against Jugurtha required more boots on the ground. The army in Numidia must have been considerably reduced in numbers, partly by casualties, partly too by the detachment of men left to garrison such strongholds as Metellus had occupied. Marius therefore spent some time in Italia enrolling new recruits. In this he took a bold step and opened the ranks to all who wished to volunteer, including the *capite censi* (head count), those citizens listed in the census simply as numbers because they lacked significant property.

Bred lean and resilient in the vicissitudes of daily survival at subsistence level, Marius would have much preferred volunteers who were members of the rural population. This was for the simple reason that such men were rightly considered to be better material for soldiering than their urban counterparts, at best a rough and undernourished lot. Yet these urbanites, the men with nothing, were willing to join for any number of reasons. While not high, there was the regular pay, and there was an ordered life, decent food and clothing, and, perhaps, the chance of improving one's lot in life. Only too grateful to escape the filth and fickleness of urban life in the underbelly of Rome, and the desire for a life free of routine drudgery all played their part in attracting the *proletarii*, poverty was the prime cause for their abandonment of civilian life. These men were enrolled in the army by Marius on his own initiative to make up the numbers in his army destined for bitter war in Africa. With Marius, the pattern was set whereupon the volunteer often linked his fortunes with his general. But as yet this lay in the future and would be a race that was a marathon, not a sprint.

What was new about Marius' dropping the property qualification for enlistment was the actuality that it was never re-imposed thereafter. This would later open the way for ambitious and unscrupulous politicians to turn the *proletarii* into their own clients with the promise of land distributions on demobilization. That is why the agrarian law passed by Caesar in 59 BC during his first consulship would cater not only for the urban poor, but also Pompeian veterans: fierce, rough, hard-bitten soldiers who just happened to be in Rome and helped to assure the passage of the bill.

Still, all this came to constitute a precedent for the future, demobilized veterans turning to their general rather than the state for their rewards of service, and – more to the point – a grant of fertile land. Simultaneously, a general turned to his demobilized veterans to support him in the cutthroat arena of politics. The reciprocated dependence of general and veterans at the conclusion of a war meant that the general would be anxious to attach to himself so many new clients, while the veterans were clearly concerned to secure for themselves as much as possible.

And so it was that volunteers from the *proletarii* of Rome chose to join the legions. For '[e]ach man fancied in his mind that he would be enriched by booty, would return home a victor, and other such visions' (*B Iug.* 84.4). Certainly, with regards to material rewards, serving under Marius in Numidia the hopes of these men were to be fulfilled (*B Iug.* 87.1, 91.6, 92.2). Meanwhile, the Senate, despite assuming that Marius would levy his soldiers by the constitutional channel of raising an army through the census-based *dilectus*, raised no protest. It was a simple step, revolutionary only in that Marius created, without realizing it, a type of client army, bound to its general as its *patronus*. In the fullness of time, this would have a cultural effect of transforming the understanding of military service from a logic based on citizenship to the logic of personal gain: service was increasingly to be conditioned on the expectation of reward.

To be sure, there had been from time to time some modifications in the recruiting system. In 123 BC, during his first rumbustious tribunate, Caius Gracchus had found it necessary to supply war gear at public cost to those recruits too poor to furnish it themselves. Besides, there had been at least three reductions in the minimum requirement to include additional men in the fifth, and lowest, income class so that more and more of the poor would be eligible for enrolment (Liv. 1.4.37 [11,000 *asses*], Polyb. 6.19.2 [4,000 *asses*], Cic. *Rep.* 2.40 [1,500 *asses*]). A military pragmatist, Marius was merely recognizing the status quo. For this reason, we need not believe that the state was scrambling for manpower anywhere it could grab it, so opening the floodgates to the destitute in the slums of the Aventine, or that the *dilectus* suddenly became obsolete overnight (Brunt 1971: 403–10, 635–68, cf. Rich 1983). That final step would have to wait until Augustus.

Marius' first campaign

Marius' army was obviously an interesting mixture of African veterans and novice soldiers. Much of the army was now experienced, having been put under discipline by Metellus and led by him with constant, if moderate, success, and they had been hardened to soldiering under an African sun. This was not the case with Marius' poor volunteers. Lacking the same stamina and steadfastness as those who had already faced the Numidians, he knew he had to break them into the Numidian war slowly. Accordingly, he exposed his soldiers, war-worn and greenhorns alike, to small fights until they were confident of themselves and the new and old hands grew easy with each other. After these preliminary preparations and opening operations, which involved largely fluid short-lived skirmishes, a spirit of teamwork henceforth prevailed among his soldiers. He was ready for a new effort against Jugurtha, who he was able to defeat in an engagement near Cirta (*B Iug.* 88.3).

However, finding that it is not so easy to end the war (with half the forces) as he had claimed

Military reenactors equipped and armed as Polybian *velites*, Gergovie plateau, Les Arverniales, 2012. Polybios (6.22.3) mentions how certain *velites* would adorn their helmets with a wolf's skin so as to be visible to their centurions from a distance; such individuals, being keen to impress, led by example. A high degree of courage would have been required in order to get close enough to use their missiles to chip away at the enemy, necessitating the need to enter the killing zone and exposing oneself as an individual to enemy fire. (Elliott Sadourny, CC BY-SA 3.0 https://creativecommons.org/licenses/by-sa/3.0, via Wikimedia Commons)

'There was in the midst of huge waste lands a large, strong town called Capsa' (*B Iug.* 89.4). When Capsa (Gafsa, Tunisia) surrendered to Marius in the late summer of 107 BC, he burned it, slew its adult males, sold the rest of the inhabitants into slavery and divided the booty among his men. The slaughter and destruction done at Marius' bidding far exceeded the needs of war. It cannot be supposed that this treatment endeared Rome to the Numidians, and was, in essence, a calculated piece of terrorism. Except for this foray towards Capsa, Marius principally campaigned in western Numidia. (Habib M'henni, CC BY-SA 3.0 https://creativecommons.org/licenses/by-sa/3.0, via Wikimedia Commons)

– rhetoric is a terrible substitute for strategy – events now took an ugly turn with Marius adopting a policy of plunder and terrorism, burning fields, villages and towns, and massacring the civilian population (*B Iug.* 91.6–7, 92.3, cf. 54.6, 55.4–6). Having left behind ashes and ruins, bloated bodies and congealed blood, Marius now conceived and planned a daring venture. This was to be a long march to surpass his predecessor's exploit at Thala and to continue to spread terror of Roman arms deep in the very heart of the hostile Numidian country. His goal was Capsa (Gafsa, Tunisia), some 483km via Sicca from Cirta. To reach it in fighting condition, supply of food and water for the army would be essential. To meet these needs, Marius ordered that cattle accompany the army; because there was only one watering place before entering the desert, which would take three days to cross before reaching Capsa, he also ordered that all the hides of butchered cattle be converted into water containers. Achieving a complete surprise – he had marched over the desert only at night and rested during the sweltering heat of the day – Marius captured Capsa, razed it, massacred the adult males, sold the rest into slavery, and divided the booty among his men. The destruction was complete.

Arguments may be concocted for viewing the massacre within the context of the time but, undeniably, it was bad business. Sallust himself calls the fate of Capsa a 'contravention of the right of war' (*contra ius belli*: *B Iug.* 91.7), but feebly excuses it as necessary since 'the place was of advantage to Jugurtha and difficult of access for us, while the character of the populace was fickle' (op. cit.). This act of calculated cruelty certainly cowed the Numidians into evacuating many of their settlements, and those few that foolishly resisted were captured by assault and razed to the ground. Cicero's later observation that 'laws are silent when arms are raised' (*Pro Milone* 11) may suggest that there was no place for the niceties of law while engaged in a primordial struggle.

Marius' second campaign

The long march to Capsa belongs late in the summer of 107 BC. Sallust is for once explicit (*B Iug*. 90.1). Marius and his army attempted to assault a fortress (*castellum*) not far from the Muluccha (Moulouya) River, perched

Oued Moulouya, Sallust's Muluccha, which formed the boundary between Numidia and Mauretania. As the Moulouya currently forms the frontier between Algeria and Morocco, there is an argument that the river in our story was much further to the east near Cirta, or Sallust has got the name wrong. It was Marius' seizure of Jugurtha's last treasury, housed in a nearby fortress, which forced the Numidian king to offer Bocchus of Mauretania a third of his kingdom in return for his aid. Significantly, Jugurtha's forces are now referred to by Sallust exclusively as Mauretanian and Gaetulian. It was the treachery of Bocchus that finally brought the war to an end. (Drissbkd, CC BY-SA 4.0 https://creativecommons.org/licenses/by-sa/4.0, via Wikimedia Commons)

BELOW LEFT
Table de Jugurtha, near Kalaat es Senam, western Tunisia, a geological feature known as an inverted relief. At an altitude of 1,255m and 1,500m long and 500m wide, the mesa stands almost 600m above the Ez-Zghalma plain and covers an area of some 80ha. Potable water comes from a local spring, the Ain Senan. (SalmaBenAissaTunisia, CC BY-SA 4.0 https://creativecommons.org/licenses/by-sa/4.0, via Wikimedia Commons)

BELOW RIGHT
The rock-cut stairway still provides access to the flat top of the mesa and its fortifications. Tradition has it that Masinissa fortified the site around 200 BC. Having entrenched himself in remote, mountainous and semi-desert terrain towards the end of his struggle with Rome, it was at remote locations such as this that Jugurtha attempted to hold off the encroaching Romans. (Camille56, CC BY-SA 4.0 https://creativecommons.org/licenses/by-sa/4.0, via Wikimedia Commons)

high upon a precipitous rock accessible only by a narrow, snaking path bordered by precipices. Sallust describes the Muluccha as the boundary dividing the realms of Jugurtha and Bocchus (*B Iug.* 92.5, also at 19.7, 110.8), which places Marius and his army far to the west of Cirta (about 800km as the crow flies) and not far from what is now Melilla (*contra* Hawthorn 1969: lv–lvi).

However that may be, and it suggests an efficient commissariat and an endless ability to march in Numidia's unforgiving geography, it was here that Marius came ever so close to losing the war. One last push – it appeared – and the Jugurtha question would be resolved. However, the long, blistering march to the Muluccha was an act of folly, which only fortune corrected (*B Iug.* 94.7). In war you need to be lucky.

The fortress' location has never been identified with certainty. Sallust does not mention an *oppidum* by name, but speaks of a broad mountain situated high enough above a river (Muluccha) to make it accessible from only one direction. The sides of this mountain were scarped and sheer; access to the plateau could only be obtained by a single difficult path; 'for the whole place was naturally steep, as if it had been made so by art and design' (*B Iug.* 92.5). The fortress, which was well garrisoned and amply supplied with provisions and water, was captured through the ploy of a Ligurum soldier finding an unguarded route and leading a chosen party up the treacherous rock face in the enemy's rear.

The Ligurum, who apparently had a passion for edible snails, went hunting for his supper. As he climbed gathering the snails, he unexpectedly found himself on the plateau at the rear of the fortress. On reporting his discovery, Marius assigned five horn blowers (*cornicines*) and trumpeters (*tubicines*) and four centurions, 'together with a few soldiers' (*B Iug.* 93.8, cf. Frontin. 3.9.3 who specifically attests a squad), to follow the fearless Ligurum back up the mountain. Their mission was to infiltrate the far side of the fortress undetected.

'After having his soldiers form the *testudo*' (*B Iug.* 94.3), Marius led a general attack at the entrance to the fortress so as to create a suitable diversion while the party clambered up the mountain and infiltrated the fortress to its rear. As Frontinus elaborates, 'These men went bareheaded and barefooted, that they might see better and make their way more easily over the rocks; their *scuta* and *gladii* were fastened to their backs. Guided by the Ligurum, and aided by straps and staffs, with which they supported themselves, they made their way up to the rear of the fortress, which owing to its position, was without defenders' (Frontin. 3.9.3).

Actually, rather than their own *scuta*, as Frontinus implies, the Romans chose to carry shields 'of Numidian design, made of hide, both because of their lighter weight and so they would make less noise if bumped' (*B Iug.* 94.1). A *scutum* would have been a cumbersome burden for a man scaling a sheer rock face, even if he was nimble as Frontinus suggests, whereas a Numidian wicker and hide shield would have been much more manageable.

Having gained access undetected, the musicians of the party sounded their instruments; the defenders lost heart believing the Romans had entered the rear of the fortress in force.

It is curious to note that while Sallust sees Marius as the living embodiment of the just qualities most precious to him, he does imply that Marius got extremely lucky on this occasion (*B Iug.* 94.7). After all, the fortress was captured, abetted by the gastronomic discernment of one Ligurum soldier serving in Marius' army,[9] and with it the largest treasury of Jugurtha. It was at this time that Sulla, Marius' *quaestor*, arrived (*B Iug.* 95.1): although the office was chiefly concerned with military finance, Sulla had been left behind in Italia to muster cavalry among the *socii*.

The reader next witnesses Marius in retreat – even Sallust's martial hero was fallible – being harassed by a cloud of Gaetulian and Mauretanian horsemen, Jugurtha and Bocchus having joined forces after the Numidian had offered to cede to the Mauretanian king one-third of his kingdom. Though the desperate fighting was 'something more like an action against bandits than a pitched battle' (*B Iug.* 97.5), Marius did manage to fight a series of set engagements towards the end of his retreat. The first was a near-run thing whereby Jugurtha was eventually surrounded and cut himself out with great difficulty, the second a sharp encounter close to Cirta, the goal of his march (*B Iug.* 101.1–11, 102.1–2), and a possible third outside the town itself (Oros. 5.15.9, who almost certainly derives from Livy). During the second engagement, another touch-and-go affair, Jugurtha attempted to

Augustan-era portrait bust traditionally identified as Sulla (Munich, Glyptothek, inv. 309). Lucius Cornelius Sulla Felix (138–78 BC) hailed from a distinguished but decayed patrician family. Unlovely as he was in his pomp, Sulla was a creature of conflict: he came across as a courteous character of cold, calculating cruelty with a reputation for devious clairvoyance and an iniquitous memory. An utterly ruthless man, this dogged dictator-to-be would callously crush all those who he believed had stood in his way or had risen up against him, Marius included. (Glyptothek, public domain, via Wikimedia Commons)

---

9   The Ligures (sg. Ligurum) inhabited the region of the Italian Peninsula known today as Liguria.

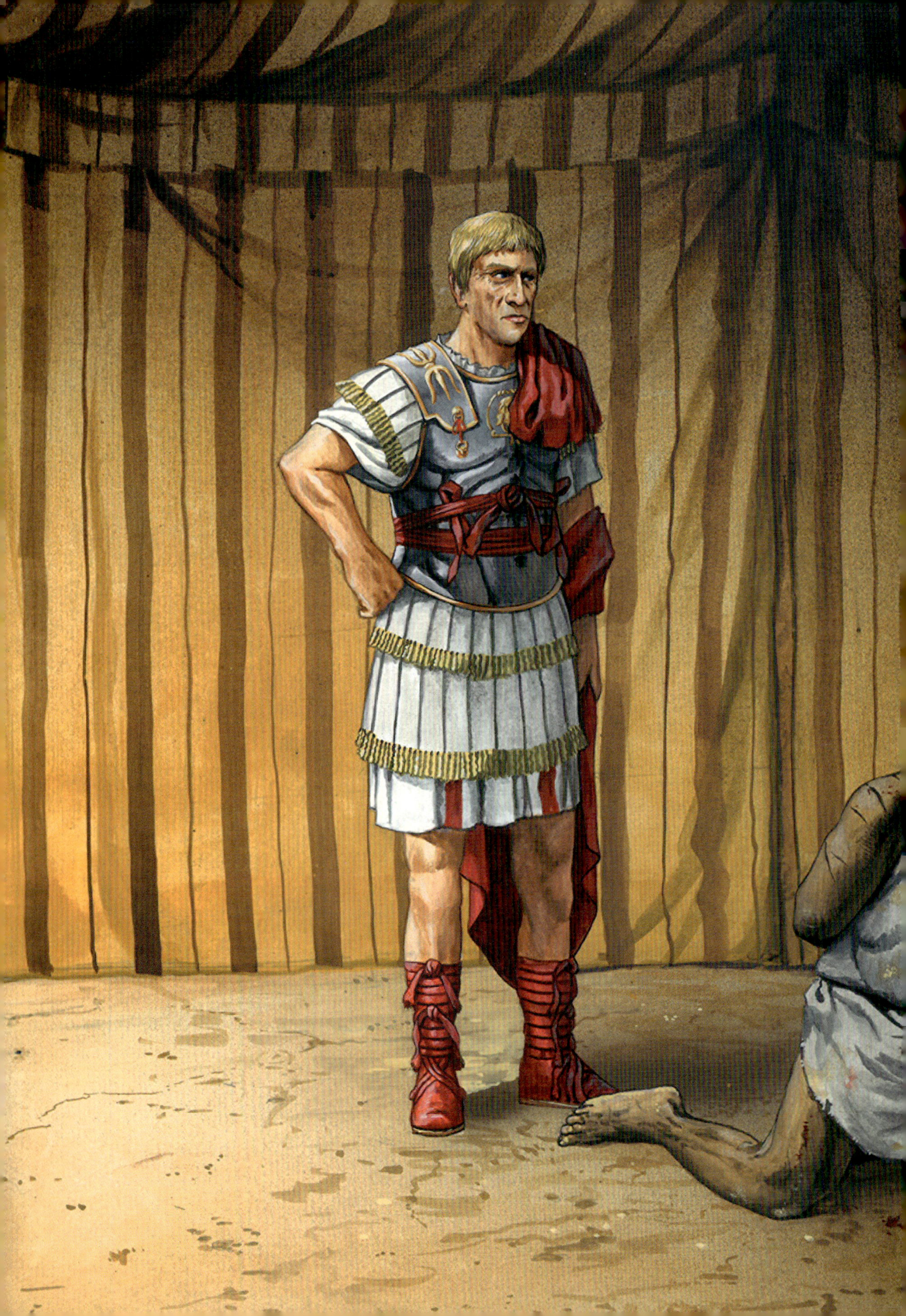

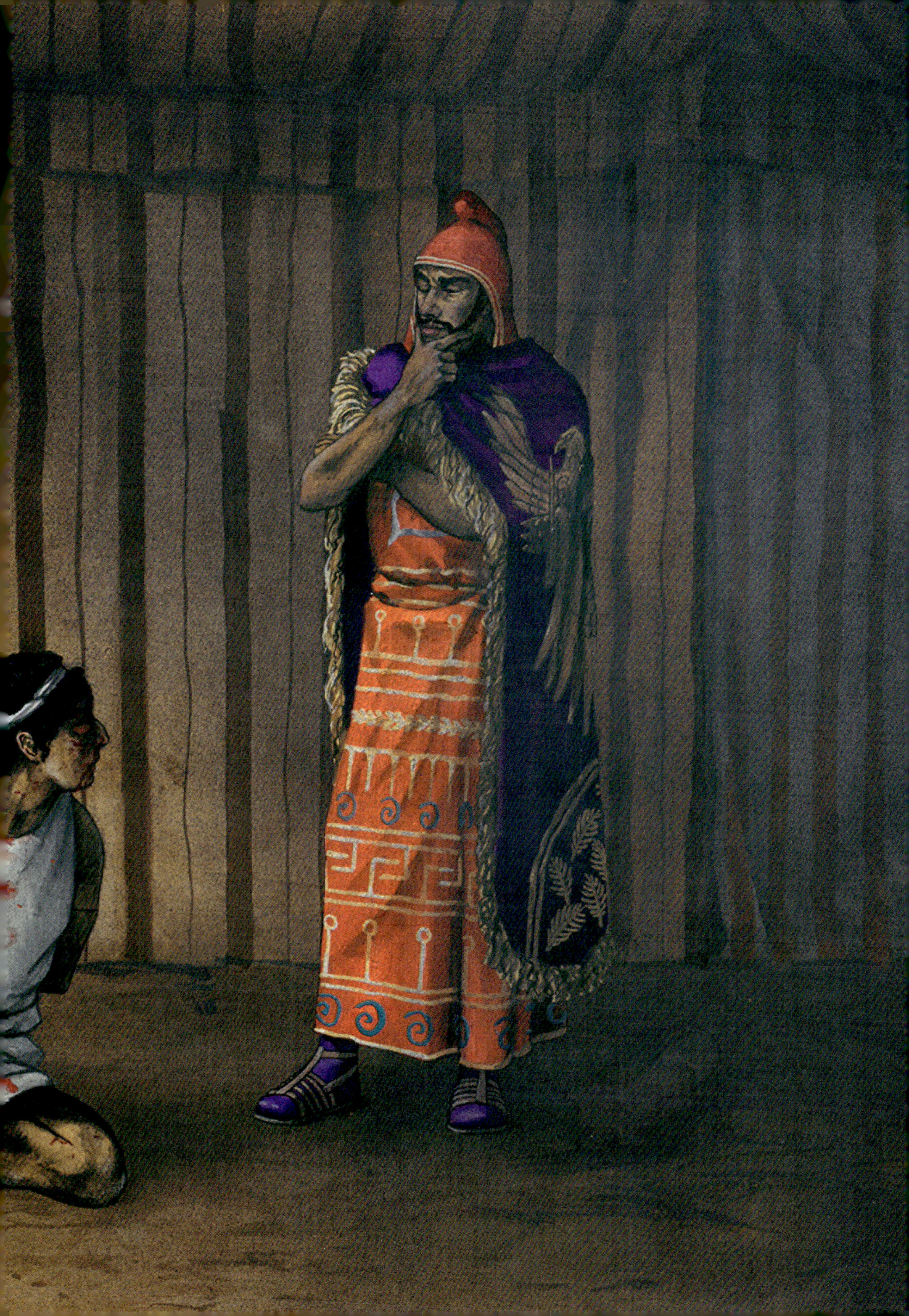

BOCCHUS BETRAYS JUGURTHA TO SULLA, 105 BC (PP.78–79)

Bocchus, king of Mauretania, had written to Marius asking that his *quaestor* Sulla be sent to discuss with him a matter of common interest to himself and Rome. Sulla set out immediately, accompanied by an escort of *equites*, a *cohors* of Balearic slingers and a *cohors* of Italian *socii* lightly equipped for hasty travel.

Jugurtha's future was trembling in the balance, when Sulla arrived at Bocchus' desert camp. The Numidian king's hour had come. The 'matter of common interest' was his betrayal. When Jugurtha attended what he was led to believe was a peace conference, his unarmed escort was cut down to the last man, and the betrayed king was given up to Sulla who, in due time, delivered him to Marius.

Everybody wants to be on the winning side. Bocchus, in spite of being the father-in-law of Jugurtha, had been hesitant about which side to support in the war. When Jugurtha lost most of his army and fled to him, Bocchus gave him shelter, but considered handing him over to the Romans. Sulla, during a private meeting with Bocchus, managed to convince him to betray Jugurtha in a planned ambush. In this reconstruction, the ambush has gone to plan and Bocchus **(1)**, now attired in his royal regalia, is handing over the bound and dishevelled Jugurtha **(2)** to Sulla, who has donned his dress uniform for the occasion albeit, because he is in the royal presence, he is unarmed **(3)**. The final betrayal takes place within the confines of Bocchus' royal tent **(4)**.

Still, on this fateful day the question lingering in Sulla's mind is how near was Bocchus to betraying him rather than his son-in-law Jugurtha? The scheming king probably made the same proposition to Jugurtha he had privately made to Sulla. If so, then Sulla's and Jugurtha's roles inside Bocchus' tent could easily have been reversed.

break the stubborn resistance of the Romans by a simple ruse. This he did by waving a bloodied sword and claiming he had personally cut down Marius: 'There, he cried out in Latin (for he had learned to speak it at Numantia) that our men were fighting in vain, that he had killed Marius with his own hand shortly before' (*B Iug.* 101.6, repeated by Frontin. 2.4.10).

At this point it should be made clear that Marius turned out to be an able commander who, though lacking the brilliance and flair of his nephew Caesar, understood the basic requirements for a good army were training, discipline and leadership. More a common soldier than an aristocratic general, it was in Numidia that he 'won the affection of the soldiers by showing he could live as hard as they did and endure as much' (Plut. *Mar.* 7.5). He was tough, unscrupulous and altogether the kind of ruffian whom the soldiers would have recognized as a man after their own hearts. Their fighting general was an old campaigner who ate what they ate, shared their hardships, and knew war as they knew it. Jugurtha certainly knew this of Marius, and it was no far-fetched claim of his when he tried to convince the Roman soldiers he had just dispatched their general. Not only was he more at ease in the rough life of the camp, Marius was personally brave too: facing the *furor Teutonicus* for the first time at the battle of Aquae Sextiae (102 BC), Marius would set a brave example to his men by positioning himself in the front rank of the fighting line (Fields 2023: 67). Still, as a tactician, Marius relied mainly on surprise and always showed a reluctance to engage in a traditional, set-piece fight. He preferred to determine the time and place and would not be hurried. And so ended a cruel summer of murder, arson, pillage and plunder.

Marius played to win on the battlefield rather than seek compromise through patient negotiations. Be that as it may, following his near reverse near the Muluccha and the bruising retreat to Cirta, the following winter and spring were a time of delicate and lengthy negotiations with the scheming Bocchus. The running fights with Marius had demolished Jugurtha's army as a fighting force, which had left the Numidian king wholly reliant upon the Mauretanian king, who had fled the fight at the first sign of difficulty and so still had his forces largely intact.

The final outcome of these on-and-off parleys with Bocchus was Sulla's seven-day journey to the king's desert camp, Sulla's near betrayal (*B Iug.* 108.3, Plut. *Mar.* 10.4, *Sull.* 3.4), culminating in Jugurtha's treacherous betrayal. The eloquent Sulla had befriended the Mauretanian king and deftly played on his ambitions and fears. And it paid off. Bocchus, now experiencing cold feet, was ready to trim his sails to the wind.

This bit of family treachery terminated a conflict full of duplicity, skirmishes and sieges. Sulla had a signet ring specially made with a seal depicting Bocchus delivering Jugurtha to him, so provoking Marius' jealousy (Val. Max. 8.14.4, Plin. 37.1.9, Plut. *Mar.* 10.5, *Sull.* 4.1, cf. *Mar.* 32.2). Nevertheless, Marius was the hero of the hour. He triumphed on 1 January 104 BC, entering on the same day his second consulship, and Jugurtha was publicly executed (*B Iug.* 113.6).

Taking the long view, the war had been a rather pointless, dirty affair without clearly defined political goals. Having started out as a war of open-ended uncertainty – humiliation, incompetence, criminality, failure – under Metellus and Marius it morphed into another one of unremitting annihilation, obliteration and destruction. As Roman generals marched

Silver *denarius* (Berlin, Münzkabinett der Staatlichen Museen, inv. 18201728) issued in 56 BC by the *triumvir monetalis* Faustus Cornelius Sulla (RRC 426–21). Obverse: draped and diademed bust of Diana, to whom Sulla paid a vow of gratitude after his victory at Mount Tifata during the civil war of 83–82 BC. Reverse: Sulla seated on a tribunal with Bocchus kneeling and offering an olive branch as a token of submission, and behind him Jugurtha on his knees with his hands bound behind his back. The legend FELIX, 'fortunate', is the honorific name Sulla awarded himself after Caius Marius Minor killed himself in 82 BC (Vell. 2.27.5, *Vir. ill.* 75, Plin. 22.12, Plut. *Sull.* 34.2). This image presumably was a reproduction of Sulla's famous seal: as dictator Sulla always sealed documents with the scene of Jugurtha being handed over to him. (Dirk Sonnenwald, Münzkabinett, Staatliche Museen zu Berlin - Stiftung Preußischer Kulturbesitz, 18201845)

about in search of a pitched battle, the wily, elusive Jugurtha who, with his firsthand knowledge of the Roman military and its lumbering armies, proved a formidable opponent: relying on speed and mobility more than anything else, Jugurtha hovers in the background, difficult to bring to ground, erupting whenever he senses an opportunity, as he did against Metellus at the Muthul. It was Metellus who realized it was useless to march pointlessly about in search of the enemy, concentrating instead on intimidating the population by attacking the towns of Numidia. Marius' strategy of fire and slaughter was that of Metellus, but with a larger area of operation, hence we find him at one point far to the west in the vicinity of the Muluccha.

In antiquity as today, tyrants tend to blunder. This they usually do by slipping on the blood they have shed: it was the killings following the fall of Cirta that provoked Roman armed intervention in Numidia. In what turned out to be a lengthy conflict, Jugurtha had given the Romans a long and aggravating chase; he had eluded them and escaped from their snares; he could not be taken or killed in battle, so the Romans finally resorted to treachery and were successful. The Jugurthine War came to an end.

Yet the war had made Marius' reputation and kick-started Sulla's belated career, though it was to be an association that never touched on amity. Worse still, it was to see Marius and Sulla fall out over who was responsible for the successful conclusion to the hostilities, an acrimonious quarrel that was to cast a long sanguinary shadow on Rome. Whereas Marius prided himself on being provincial, his so-to-be bitterest foe Sulla was a patrician – not merely an aristocrat or a noble – in spite of his branch of the Cornelii having long fallen into obscurity and straitened circumstances. Rome differed significantly from modern states in legally requiring its political leaders to complete military service. Sulla had entered the arena relatively late in his life, indeed first performing military service as Marius' *quaestor* in Numidia (Plut. *Mar.* 10.3, *Sull.* 3.1). At this point of his life, Sulla stood at a fork: he either struggled towards his destiny or staggered towards the trapdoor. Obviously, we know which path he took, and it was this intense, explosive rivalry between the provincial *novus homo* and the patrician *noblis* that was rhapsodized by Plutarch, who, it must be said, had little good to say about Marius.[10]

---

10 On numerous occasions Plutarch (*Mar.* 25.4–5, 26.3–4, 35.3, *Sull.* 4.3, 6.5, 6, 14.2, 6, 17.1, 23.2, 28.8, 37.1) says he consulted Sulla's *Memoirs*, which unfortunately has not been preserved.

SALLUST'S DISTANT, DIRTY WAR

It was commonplace among Roman historians to contrast the vitality of early Rome with the degenerate, self-destructive Rome of their own age. In the preface to his *Bellum Catilinae*, his first extant historical monograph, Sallust has much to say of the contrast between the virtuous Romans of a bygone age and the depravity of their successors. No doubt he exaggerates it, like other sermonizers on similar themes. Yet for Sallust, the

Contemporary bronze of Caius Sallustius Crispus, Piazza Palazzo, L'Aquila, Abruzzo. Sallust was born in 86 BC at Amiternum (some 9km from L'Aquila) in the territory of the Sabines. Tribune of the plebs in 52 BC, he made himself conspicuous by his turbulent conduct in connection with the trial of the political agitator Titus Annius Milo (an implacable enemy of Sallust) for the murder of the demagogue Publius Clodius Pulcher (Ascon. 37C.18–21). Two years later, his name was struck off the roll of the Senate by the censors on the ground of his licentious life (Dio 40.63.4). On the outbreak of the civil war in the following year, he espoused the cause of Caesar and was rewarded with the praetorship, and so back into the Senate (ibid. 45.52.2). He served under Caesar during his African campaign (47–46 BC). On the death of Caesar, he retired from public life to devote himself to historiography until his death in 35 BC. (Freegiampi, CC BY-SA 2.5 https://creativecommons.org/licenses/by-sa/2.5, via Wikimedia Commons)

Manuscript (Harvard University, Houghton Library, MS Richardson 17) c. 1490 of Sallust's *Bellum Iugurthinum*. At the time of his death, Sallust was undoubtedly without a peer among the historians of Rome, while a century or so later the poet Martial (14.191) and the critic Quintilianus (*Inst. or.* 2.5.19) still spoke of him as *primus* among Roman historians. There are few modern critics who would place him on the same level as Livy, but his gifts were great and unquestionable. (Houghton Library, public domain, via Wikimedia Commons)

grim pallbearer for the slow, rattling demise of the Roman Republic, the decisive turning point in Roman moral development was the final destruction of Rome's arch-rival, Carthage, and the consequential removal of what the historian gloomily labels 'fear of the enemy abroad' (*B Iug.* 41.2). Besides, the Punic wars and the Carthaginians provide several of Sallust's examples of heroic figures of the past (*B Iug.* 4.5, 5.4, 14.5, 14.8–10, 42.1, 79), with whom the degenerates of the present are to be contrasted.

This belief was the pessimism that domestic tranquillity depended on the fear of a strong external threat, that is to say, the Romans, nobility and people alike, would remain united in self-defence and their civil affairs would remain peaceful as a result. For Sallust, as for many of his forbearers and successors, superpower rivalry was fundamentally a two-tier game, and it was impossible to disentangle a state's domestic values from its foreign policy. Actions in one domain inevitably bled into the other: in a revealing comment, Polybios (32.13.6–8) reports that the Senate feared the army would lose its fighting edge if it were not used. The alternative was obvious; the citizens would turn their energies to unrestrained and violently destructive rivalries among themselves (Harris 1986: 127–8, 266–7).

The *Bellum Iugurthinum*, the second of Sallust's extant historical monographs, explores the intertwined themes of Rome's war in Africa and the concomitant political upheavals in Rome. Yet the *Bellum Iugurthinum* is more than a biography of Jugurtha. It is a narration of an international war that impinges on the internal politics of Rome, with dire and distant repercussions.

Through the eyes of our epoch, the *Bellum Iugurthinum* presents a stimulating study replete with chilling modern resonance: a superpower lacking the sufficient political and moral guidance; an unstable political system in a marginal state; the superpower's patronage of the local rulers; acts of violence against the superpower's local representatives who are reinforcing its economic interests; a dirty war fought in arid wastes with no clear aim or exit strategy; and civil unrest within the superpower caused by the failure of those responsible and by their enemy's underhand agitation. No matter the epoch, military operations can be greatly hampered by political intransigence and lack of positive identification of missions and roles. For Sallust, the failure in the war against Jugurtha was primarily down to the corruption of senatorial virtue by ambition and greed.

Moving from the wide-ranging to the particular, Sallust does have things to say: about how the Jugurthine War was responsible for setting in motion the subsequent period of internal political conflict between the various senatorial generals and the deep division between the *nobiles* and the *novi homines*, all of which culminated in the civil wars of the following century. The first of these of course was the acrimonious contest between Marius and Sulla, a time which was marked by the marching and counter-marching of Roman armies, by chaos, by muddled loyalties and by harsh reckonings meted out to opponents.

A staunch supporter of Caesar, Sallust had served under him during the civil war of 49–45 BC. Anti-senatorial, he was one of the late Republic's most pungent observers of domestic polarization and decline as well as its most forceful political moralist. Blame was the point for Sallust, and let the blame begin here, said he, now that the truth is known. As for the facts of the matter, Sallust's elucidation was simple: bribery (*B Iug.* 13.5–8, 15.1, 3, 15.5–16.1, 16.3–4, 20.1, 29.1–3). Bribes, of course, are dangerous; they have the habit of growing larger and larger. True, Jugurtha must have possessed a considerable amount of personal wealth – he was capable of paying Metellus an indemnity of 200,000 pounds of silver (*B Iug.* 62.5) – but it is probably wise not to follow Sallust too closely in jumping to indiscreet conclusions.

Take, for example, the pandemonium that broke out when a tribune-designate and a dogged enemy of the ruling oligarchy, Caius Memmius, who is described by Sallust as 'an energetic man hostile to the power of the *nobilitas*' (*B Iug.* 27.2), turns the war into a political issue, using it as a weapon with which to attack the Senate. Given the fact that the Numidian 'villain' was still at large, somebody must be fixed for the blame. So, assuming we are in the business of making moral judgements of this kind, who are we going to point the finger at?

All the men currently pre-eminent in the Senate are those who

Portrait bust traditionally identified as Caius Marius (Vaticani, Museo Chiaramonti, inv. 1488), 1st century BC. Marius held a total of seven consulships, unequalled by any Roman before Augustus. Yet fighting not politics was his first desideratum, and Marius brought to a close the Jugurthine War, and later the more serious threat to Italia from migrating Cimbri and Teutones. His significance in history is as a *novus homo* who succeeded in war but failed in politics: a man of action, not of words, intolerant under restraint, unprincipled when frustrated. (Vatican Museums, CC BY 3.0 https://creativecommons.org/licenses/by/3.0, via Wikimedia Commons)

had opposed the Gracchi brothers – those honest men from the ranks of the *nobilitas* who had championed the people and, for their troubles, had fallen victims of violence – and were involved in the cruel repression of their popular reforms and supporters.

There is no evidence that Memmius had anything positive to offer with regard to the actual conduct of the war: his intervention was purely negative. Whether or not there were those who aided and abetted Jugurtha, he saw a small chink in the armour of the Senate, which had no shortage of enemies. Its attacks on the tribunate had not won it any favours with the people.

Two years later, another tribune of the plebs, Caius Mamilius Limetanus, proposed to the *concilium plebis* that a court, *quaestio Mamiliana*, should be set up in order to prosecute those senators who, so it was alleged, had favoured Jugurtha in any shape or form. Predictably, Sallust, a careful contriver, concerns himself with those senators who had either 'accepted money from him while serving as envoys or commanders, those who had handed back elephants and deserters, likewise those who had concluded with the enemy concerning peace or war' (*B Iug.* 40.1). Much to the discomfiture of the Senate, five prominent men, four of consular rank and one a holder of an unnamed priesthood, were eventually convicted, so paying the penalty for what they had done (or not done) in Numidia (*B Iug.* 65.5).

The *quaestio Mamiliana* was essentially a settling of old scores, an act of vengeance for the deaths of the Gracchi. That was the whole and simple truth. So, it was not a good time to be a senator, especially if you happened to be one of the five condemned by the *quaestio Mamiliana*, who are named by Cicero (*Brut.* 127–8). The names are not without interest.

Lucius Opimius (*cos.* 121 BC) was the prime target of the *quaestio Mamiliana* – as Sallust points out, he was the head of the senatorial commission to partition Numidia between Jugurtha and Adherbal. Moreover, this hard-headed reactionary had gained notoriety for his part in orchestrating the purge of Caius Gracchus and his supporters (Plut. *C. Gracch.* 18.1, cf. *B Iug.* 16.2) – the crime was never punished, arrogance and cruelty prevailed.

Lucius Calpurnius Bestia (*cos.* 111 BC), who began the war and came to an agreement with Jugurtha, was one of the tribunes of the plebs for 121 BC when he had passed a motion allowing Publius Popillius Laenas (*cos.* 132 BC) to be recalled from exile: it was Laenas who had dealt with the surviving supporters of Tiberius Gracchus and for that had been exiled by Caius Gracchus, tribune in succession to his murdered brother.

Regrettably we do not know the connection of the two Gracchi with the other three convicted men named by Cicero: Caius Porcius Cato (*cos.* 114 BC), Spurius Postumius Albinus (*cos.* 110 BC) and Caius Sulpicius Galba, a patrician and holder of an unspecified priesthood. The Gracchi brothers were dead, to be sure; but their ideals and aspirations were to influence the political activities of Romans for almost a century to come.

As interesting as are the names on Cicero's list, there is one that is absent. Marcus Aemilius Scaurus, clearly sensing how the wind was blowing, in a remarkable pirouette got himself appointed as one of the three members of the *quaestio Mamiliana* (*B Iug.* 40.4). Whether the tribune's purpose was well meaning, the intention behind it was the classic conjurer's misdirection. At its heart, this was not a political dispute about bribery and corruption, but power: who gets to wield it, how they keep it and who gets to hold it accountable. So, the conduct of Numidian affairs merely presented an excuse and an opportunity. As the magisterial Syme once put it, 'It is strange that Sallust now neglected this signal act of justice and revenge' (2002: 168).

Strange it may be, but Sallust saw, albeit with a more than slightly jaundiced eye, the Jugurthine War as marking a fundamental phase in the decline of the self-satisfied senatorial oligarchy and the orchestration of the attack upon it (see *B Iug.* 5.1–2). In particular, domestic and foreign affairs, the prerogative of the Senate, were increasingly irrigated by a brackish flow of illicit funds and dark money, something Sallust chronicles remarkably effectively in *Bellum Iugurthinum*.

Without a doubt, Jugurtha was a monstrously ambitious creature, using the trappings of the Roman world where it suited him and speaking Latin. Of course, he was more of a manipulator than an appreciator: he would cultivate Roman acquaintances without the need of being truly affable. Beyond bribery of course it could have been a classic case of procrastination and thumb sucking on the senators' part. After all, Rome at this time was not the arch imperialist with its perennial colonialist instincts.

Naturally, Sallust sees the constant failure to overcome Jugurtha as partly incompetence but primarily down to the moral corruption of the Roman aristocracy: Rome, for him at least, was a society past its prime, assailed by foes within and without. The *Bellum Iugurthinum* reads like a standard text on diplomatic and military failure, and Sallust seems at his happiest when sharing with dour satisfaction the catalogue of woes with his readership. In this regard, he portrays the chief villain of his monologue, Jugurtha, both as the 'noble savage', immune against the corruption of a failing Roman civilization, and as the 'ignoble barbarian', a paradigm of 'Punic' perfidy. Sallust seems to have despised him and revered him in equal measure.

We can of course take a sceptic's stance over the fallibility of such a partisan and hyperbolic account by a historian with several axes to grind. It was like this. Sallust, with the benefit of hindsight, would see this as a power struggle, where one power, the aristocratic Senate, which believes it has an immutable mandate, wants to suck the air out of the other, the populist tribunate, which is hitting back, and it is hitting where it hurts. We may quibble with some of Sallust's conclusions, but to be fair to him, we should appreciate that one of the sources for his monograph was the forensic speeches from the judicial examinations of those five condemned *nobiles*. Sallust did not provide the gloss himself.

Sallust takes pains to demonstrate how Roman military performance was hampered by petty rivalries, knee-jerk partisanship and grubby jostling between senatorial generals. The fact that the war occurs on formerly Carthaginian territory also lends it a depressing kaleidoscopic quality – immediately conjuring up unflattering comparisons with the celebrated wars fought by two generations of Rome's foremost family, the Cornelii Scipiones, across the same sun-scorched scenery. The Jugurthine War was a terrible war, and it would leave scars that refused to heal.

AFTERMATH

Academics tend to work on history's successes, and Jugurtha, once declared an enemy of the state, was heading for oblivion. Sallust, on the other hand, made the story of the Numidian villain-hero into a tragedy: pride and overconfidence, that form of narcissism described in Greek tragedies that invariably led to the great fall. He obviously took a delight in his use of the language of the theatre, confidently writing without the perpetual niggling 'perhaps' or 'although' to which we moderns are condemned. Anyone who has read *Hamlet* knows that you become what you pretend you are. People die; a kingdom was ruined. As so it proved. In the body-strewn Shakespearean play of Jugurtha's short-lived reign, we are into the last act.

Still, Jugurtha, for sheer tenacity and iron courage, deserved a better fate than was eventually accorded him by Rome. The king was paraded in chains through the streets of Rome mockingly attired in his royal robes. The final act of the tragedy shall be told by Plutarch:

> It is said that, when he was led before the car of the conqueror, he lost his reason. After the triumph he was thrown into prison, where, while they were in haste to strip him, some tore his robe off his back, and others snatching at his ear-rings, pulled off the tips of his ears with them. When he was thrust naked into the dungeon, all wild and confused, he said with a frantic smile, 'Heavens! How cold is this bath of yours!' There, struggling for six days with the last pangs of hunger, and to the last hour labouring for the preservation of his life, he came to such an end as his life deserved. (Plut. *Mar.* 12.3–4)

BELOW RIGHT
The hole, now fitted with an iron grille, gave access to the lower cell where Jugurtha was incarcerated before his execution (as implied by Sallust), though this plaque (following Plutarch) says he 'died from starvation'. (J. van Rooden, public domain, via Wikimedia Commons)

BELOW LEFT
Marble plaque, Carcere Mamertino, listing the names in Italian of some of the illustrious inmates incarcerated there and how they met their terrible ends: Jugurtha is the fourth name on the list. The prison was known as the Tullianum (Fest. 490L) and held criminals and captives awaiting their execution. It took the form of a dungeon, which had two subterranean cells, one on top of the other. The lower cell was located within the sewer system and could only be reached by being lowered through a hole in the floor of the upper cell. The Tullianum was located on the Clivus Argentarius just below the Capitoline. (Lalupa, CC BY-SA 3.0 http://creativecommons.org/licenses/by-sa/3.0/, via Wikimedia Commons)

Sallust, however, implies Jugurtha was publicly executed (*B Iug.* 114.3), perhaps by the garrotte (see Luc. 9.600: 'breaking of the neck of Jugurtha'), during the climax of Marius' triumph. *Sic transit gloria.*

The war was brought to a close by the capture rather than the defeat of Jugurtha in 105 BC, and if the Senate chose to annexe Numidia, then the army would have to contend with Numidian tribesmen, not to mention Bocchus and the Mauretanians. Even if such an issue was even discussed in the Senate, by the time Jugurtha was in chains, the startling news of the overwhelming disaster at Arausio had already arrived in Rome, or was very soon to arrive. According to Sallust, '*Per idem tempus* [as the capture of Jugurtha]' (*B Iug.* 114.1), the battle of Arausio was fought, a disaster which took place 'one day before the nones of October' (Plut. *Lucull.* 27.7).[11] With the whole of Italia in the grip of fear, 'Marius was elected consul in his absence, and Gaul was assigned him as his province' (*B Iug.* 114.3): his election *in absentia* was of course contrary to constitutional law (Plut. *Mar.* 12.1).

The Senate did not annexe Numidia, giving instead half of its territory to Bocchus, as a reward for his treachery, and half to Gauda, the half-witted half-brother of Jugurtha (Gsell 1930: 264). This should not be seen as evidence of the Senate's pacifism but of its sound military and political sense. As Harris points out, there was no particular Roman reluctance to annex territory in this period, quite the contrary in fact, but it seems that Numidia was 'an exceptionally unattractive prospect as a province' (1986: 151). In other words, the Senate, seeing only a wasteland good for very little except subsistence farming and grazing, but which would have to be defended nonetheless, refused to annex it (there may be a lesson here for us today). The difficulties of holding such a vast domain, inhabited by a stubborn pastoral society, which was considered a cause of trouble and lawlessness by the Senate, was a sufficient deterrent, while peaceful penetration by Italian traders was a surer and more profitable policy.

As Sallust says of the situation in Vaga, 'many mortals of Italic stock had become accustomed to dwell and trade' (*B Iug.* 47.1). Direct beneficiaries of the exploitation of the growing empire were those bankers and commercial entrepreneurs, the *publicani*, who took advantage of the fact that it was impossible for members of the senatorial order overtly to obtain money by usury or commercial speculation, as stipulated by the *lex Claudia* of 218 BC. Such activity in fact contradicted the system of aristocratic standards on which their prestige and authority relied. It was certainly not due to lack of keenness on their part. But since they were unable to get rich (or richer)

Trionfo di Mario (New York, Metropolitan Museum of Art, inv. 65.183.1), oil on canvas (1725–29) by Giovanni Battista Tiepolo (1696–1770). Painted to decorate the *salone* of the Ca' Dolfin, Rio di Ca' Foscari, Venice, the Latin inscription on the banderol reads 'The Roman people saw Jugurtha led in triumph loaded with chains', a line from Florus (1.36.17). Jugurtha, who fixes the viewer with his proud stare, is shown ahead of his captor Marius, the main attraction of the latter's triumph held on 1 January 104 BC. Plutarch (*Mar.* 12.6) states that the booty amounted to 3,007 pounds of gold, 5,775 pounds of silver bullion and 287,000 *drakhmae* (= *denarii*) in minted coin. (Rogers Fund, 1965, Metropolitan Museum of Art)

---

11 The nones of October fell on the 7th, placing the battle on 6 October 105 BC.

directly by these means, they were obliged to deal through associates who represented them in all matters, even the shadiest, in which they had interests. So, there were bankers, usurers, ship owners, large and small commercial entrepreneurs who dealt in grain, olive oil, wine or slaves, and the *negotiatores* whose numbers and importance always increased, who spread through the provinces as early as the 2nd century BC. These individuals did not need any specific civic qualifications as they looked after functions that had no direct relationship with the management of the state's interests. They might or might not be Roman citizens, that is to say of the *ordo equester* (e.g. *B Iug.* 65.4), and there were many Italians among them. Thus, we find in the pages of Sallust Italian traders not only in Cirta and Vaga, but in Utica too (*B Iug.* 64.5).

As a result, two Mauretanian kingdoms emerge, separated by the River Muluccha (Plin. 5.19), and at the time of Caesar's campaign in Africa, eastern Mauretania was ruled by a second Bocchus, who, along with the Campanian *condottiere*, Publius Sittius, invaded Numidia and captured Cirta in 46 BC ([Caes.] *B Afr.* 25.2). Having rendered signal service to him, Caesar was to give the territory around Cirta to Sittius as a land-grant, who then ruled there like a client king: Sittius was to be killed by a Numidian princeling soon after the Ides of March (Cic. *Att.* 15.17.1). With the intervention of Numidia in the civil war – it opted for Pompeius and the cause of the Republic – its territory was markedly reduced in size, the most developed part east of the Ampsaga (Rhumel) River being annexed by Rome. Renamed Africa Nova, Sallust was dispatched to be its first governor, which included the command of three legions ([Caes.] *B Afr.* 97.1, App. *B civ.* 2 §100). This was the high point of Sallust's political career, but within a year it ended in ignominy: upon returning to Rome, he was thrown out of the Senate for a second time, accused of extortion and of plundering his province (Dio 43.9.2).

Marble portrait bust (Paris, Musée du Louvre, inv. Ma 1885 / MNC 1920) of Juba I of Numidia (r. 60–46 BC), represented as Jupiter, found in 1882 at Cherchell, Algeria (Cæsarea Mauretaniae). Grossly insulted by Caesar, loyal ally to Pompeius Magnus – he had restored his father Hiempsal II (r. 88–81 BC, 80–60 BC) to the throne – Juba was to commit suicide after the Pompeian defeat at Thapsus (7 February 46 BC). Following the overthrow of Juba and his senatorial allies, Sallust was appointed *pro consule* of Africa Nova (eastern Numidia) (Dio 43.47.2, 4, Gell. 17.18.1). (© Esther Carré)

North Africa at the time of Sallust's governship

FURTHER READING

Ardent du Picq, C., (trans. Col. J. Greely and Maj. R. Cotton, 1920; repr. 2006), *Battle Studies: Ancient and Modern*, Harrisburg, PA: US Army War College (1903)
Badian, E., 'From the Gracchi to Sulla', *Historia* 11: 214–28 (1962)
Bell, M. J. V., 'Tactical reform in the Roman republican army', *Historia* 14: 404–22 (1965)
Berthier, A., *La Numidie: Rome et le Maghreb*, Paris: Éditions Picard (1981)
Biglino, F., 'Rethinking second-century BC military service: the speech of Spurius Ligustinus', *Journal of Ancient History* 8/2: 208–28 (2020)
Bishop, M. C. and Coulston, J. C. N., *Roman Military Equipment from the Punic Wars to the Fall of Rome*, London: Batsford (1993)
Bonnell, F., 'Monument gréco-punique de la Soumaâ (près Constantine)', *Recueil des Notices et Mémoires de la Société archéologique de Constantine* 49: 167–78 (1915)
Brett, M. and Fentress, E. W. B, *The Berbers*, Oxford: Blackwell Publishing (1996, 1997)
Brunt, P. A., *Italian Manpower 225 BC–AD 14*, Oxford: Oxford University Press (1971, 2001)
Campbell, D. B., 'A succession of sieges: Marius and the war with Jugurtha', *Ancient Warfare Magazine* 5/1: 37–41 (2011)
Camps, G., 'Aux origins de la Bérberie: Massinissa ou les débuts de l'histoire', *Libyca archéologie-épigraphie* 8: 1–320 (1960)
Canter, H. V., 'The chronology of Sallust's *Jugurtha*', *Classical Journal* 6/7: 290–95 (1911)
Carney, T. F., *A Biography of C. Marius*, Chicago, IL: Argonaut (1962, 1970)
Cascarino, G., *L'esercito romano: armamento e organizzazione. Vol. I: dalle origini alla fine della republica*, Rimini: il Cerchio iniziative editoriali (2007)
Charles, M. B., 'African forest elephants and turrets in the ancient world', *Phoenix* 62 (3/4): 338–62 (2008)
Charles, M. B., 'The African elephants of antiquity revisited: habitat and representational evidence', *Historia* 69 (4): 392–407 (2020)
Claassen, J.-M., 'Sallust's Jugurtha – rebel or freedom fighter?: on crossing crocodile-infested waters', *Classical World* 86: 273–97 (1992–93)
Connolly, P., 'The Roman fighting technique deduced from armour and weaponry', in V. A. Maxfield and M. J. Dobson (eds), *Roman Frontier Studies: Proceeding of the Fifteenth International Congress of Roman Frontier Studies*, Exeter: Exeter University Press, 358–63 (1991)
Connolly, P., '*Pilum, gladius* and *pugio* in the late Republic', *Journal of Roman Equipment Studies* 8: 41–57 (1997)
Cornell, T. J., *The Beginnings of Rome*, London: Routledge (1995)
Delbrück, H., (trans. W. J. Renfroe), *History of the Art of War within the Framework of Political History*, vol. 1, Westport, CT: Greenwood Press (1975)
Dobson, M. J., *The Army of the Roman Republic: the Second Century BC, Polybios and the Camps at Numantia, Spain*, Oxford: Oxbow Books (2008, 2016)
Earl, D. C., 'Sallust and the Senates' Numidian policy', *Latomus* 24/3: 532–36 (1965)
Evans, R. J., *Gaius Marius: A Political Biography*, Pretoria: University of South Africa Press (1994)
Fentress, E. W. B., *Numidia and the Roman Army: Social, Military and Economic Aspects of the Frontier Zone*, Oxford: British Archaeological Reports (BAR International Series 53) (1979)
Feugère, M., *Les armes romains de la république à l'antiquité tardive*, Paris: Éditions du Centre national de la recherché scientifique (1993)

Fields, N., *The Roman Army of the Punic Wars 264–146 BC*, Oxford: Osprey Publishing (Battle Orders 27) (2007)
Fields, N., *Warlords of Republican Rome: Caesar versus Pompey*, Barnsley: Pen & Sword Military (2008) [2008A]
Fields, N., *Tarentine Horsemen of Magna Graecia 430–190 BC*, Oxford: Osprey Publishing (Warrior 130) (2008) [2008B]
Fields, N., *Roman Battle Tactics 390–110 BC*, Oxford: Osprey Publishing (Elite 172) (2010)
Fields, N., *Roman Conquests: North Africa*, Barnsley: Pen & Sword Military (2011)
Fields, N., *Roman Republican Legionary 298–105 BC*, Oxford: Osprey Publishing (Warrior 162) (2012)
Fields, N., *The Cimbrian War 113–101 BC: The Rise of Caius Marius*, Oxford: Osprey Publishing (Campaign 393) (2023)
Gabba, E., *Republican Rome: the Army and the Allies*, Oxford: Clarendon Press (1976)
Gabriel, R. and Metz, K., *From Sumer to Rome: the Military Capabilities of Ancient Armies*, Westport, CT: Greenwood Press (1991)
Gsell, S., *Histoire ancienne de l'Afrique du Nord*, tome 8, Paris: Librairie Hachette (1930)
Harris, W. V., *War and Imperialism in Republican Rome 327–70 BC*, Oxford: Clarendon Press (1979, 1986)
Hawthorn, J. R., *Rome and Jugurtha*, London: Macmillan (1969)
Hildinger, E., *Swords against the Senate: the Rise of the Roman Army and the Fall of the Republic*, Cambridge, MA: Da Capo Press (2002)
Holroyd, M., 'The Jugurthine War: was Marius or Metellus the real victor?', *Journal of Roman Studies* 18/1: 1–20 (1928)
Hopkins, K., *Conquerors and Slaves*, Cambridge: Cambridge University Press (1978)
Horsted, W., *The Numidians 300 BC–AD 300*, Oxford: Osprey Publishing (Men-at-Arms 537) (2021)
Horvat, J., 'The hoard of Roman Republican weapon from Grad near Šmihel', *Arheološki vestnik* 53: 117–92 (2002)
Hoyos, D., *A Roman Army Reader*, Mundelein: Bolchazy-Carducci (2013)
Hyden, M., *Gaius Marius: the Rise and Fall of Rome's Saviour*, Barnsley: Pen & Sword Military (2017)
Hyland, A., *Equus: the Horse in the Roman World*, London: Batsford (1990)
Kaus, C. S., 'Jugurthine disorder', in C. S. Kaus (ed.), *The Limits of Historiography: Genre and Narrative in Ancient Historical Texts*, Leiden/Boston/Köln: Brill, 217–48 (1999)
Keaveney, A., *Sulla: the Last Republican* (2nd edn), London: Routledge (2005)
Keppie, L. J. F., *The Making of the Roman Army: From Republic to Empire*, London: Routledge (1984, 1998)
Kildahl, P. A., *Caius Marius*, New York, NY: Twayne Publishers (Rulers and Statesmen of the World 7) (1968)
de Kistler, J. M., *War Elephants*, Westport, CT: Praeger Publishers (2005)
Law, R. C. C., 'The Berber kingdoms in North Africa', in J. D. Fage (ed.), *Cambridge History of Africa*, vol. 2, Cambridge: Cambridge University Press, 176–91 (1978)
Laporte, J. P., 'Stèles libyques et libyco-romaines de Kabylie (wilaya de Bejaia, Algérie)', *Bulletin archéologique du Comité des travaux historiques et scientifiques* 38: 225–26 (2018)
López García, I., 'La iconografía de la *Hispania Ulterior*: El relieve de los Soldadas de Estepa (Sevilla)', *Baetica. Estudios de Arte, Geografía e Historia* 31: 167–81 (2009)
Montgomery, P. A., 'Sallust's Scipio: a preview of aristocratic *superbia* (Sal. *Jug.* 7.2–9.2)', *Classical Journal* 109/1: 21–40 (2013)
Rawson, E. D., 'The literary sources for the pre-Marian Roman army', *Papers for the British School at Rome* 39: 13–31 (1971), republished in *Roman Culture and Society*, Oxford: 34–57 (1991)
Rich, J. W., 'The supposed manpower shortage of the later second century BC'. *Historia* 22: 287–331 (1983)
Richard, J.-C., 'La victoire de Marius', *Melanges d'archéologie et l'histoire* 77: 69–86 (1965)
Rostovtzeff, M., 'Numidian horsemen on Canosa vases', *American Journal of Archaeology* 50: 263–67 (1946)
Roth, J. P., *Roman Warfare*, Cambridge: Cambridge University Press (2009)
Sage, M., *The Republican Roman Army: a Sourcebook*, London: Routledge (2008)
Santangelo, F., *Marius*, London: Bloomsbury Academic (Ancients in Action) (2016)
Scanlon, T. F., 'Textual geography in Sallust's *The War with Jugurtha*', *Ramus: Critical Studies in Greek and Roman Literature* 17/2: 138–75 (1988)

Scullard, H. H., *The Elephant in the Greek and Roman World*, London: Thames & Hudson (1974)

Syme, R., *The Roman Revolution*, Oxford: Clarendon Press (1939, 1956)

Syme, R., *Sallust*, Berkeley/Los Angeles, CA: University of California Press (1964, 2002)

Taylor, M. J., 'Roman infantry tactics in the mid-Republic: a reassessment', *Historia* 63: 301–22 (2014)

Taylor, M. J., 'The battle scene on Aemilius Paullus's Pydna Monument: a re-evaluation', *Hesperia* 85: 559–76 (2016)

Ulbert, G., 'Das schwert und die eisernen wurfgeschoßspitzen aus dem grab von Es Soumaâ', in H. Horn and B. Ruger (eds), *Die Numider: Reiter und Könige nördlich der Sahara*, Bonn: Rheinisches Landesmuseum Bonn, 333–38 (1979)

Walbank, F. W., *A Historical Commentary on Polybios*, vol. 1, Oxford: Clarendon Press (1957)

Waurick, G., 'Die schutzwaffen im numidischen grab von Es Soumaâ', in H. Horn and B. Ruger (eds), *Die Numider: Reiter und Könige nördlich der Sahara*, Bonn: Rheinisches Landesmuseum Bonn, 305–32 (1979)

Zhmodikov, A., 'Roman Republican heavy infantryman in battle (IV–II centuries BC)', *Historia* 49: 67–78 (2000)

Jugurtha, King of Numidia, Thrown from his Roman Prison into the Tiber (Los Angeles, J. Paul Getty Museum, inv. Ms, fol. 170, 96.MR.17.170) by Boucicaut Master (fl. 1390–1430), from a French illuminated manuscript dated 1413–15. Whether Jugurtha's miserable ending was to be publically strangled or whether he was left to simply starve to death in prison, his princely corpse would have suffered the humiliation of being thrown into the Tiber, the fate of those deemed criminals by Rome. (Digital image courtesy of Getty's Open Content Program)

INDEX

Figures in **bold** refer to illustrations.

Adherbal 11, 15, 42, 43, 44, 45, **45**, 47
administrative governance 6, 16–17, 43
aedileship 20
Aelianus 22
agricultural practice 9–10
Albinus, Aulus Postumius 11, 48, 49, 50–51, **52**
Albinus, Spurius Postumius 11, 47, 48, 86
Altar of Domitius Ahenobarbus 34, **41**
Ampsaga river, Algeria 8
Appianus 22
Arcobarzanes 9
armour 32, 33, 36, 40, **40**, 41
 iron mailshirt **26**, 27
 ring mail 26, **32**
 shields 53, 77
  scutum (body shield) 32–33, **34**, 39, **40**, 77
Arrianus 32
Ateban **10**

Barb horse **19**
Barca, Hannibal 5, 6, 16, 21, 28, 31
Battle of Aquae Sextiae (102 BC) 39, 81
Battle of Arausio (105 BC) 39, 89
Battle of Muthul (109 BC) 11, 23, **54**, 57, 57–64, **58–59**, **62–63**, **66–67**, 68
Battle of Wadi Mallaq (109 BC) 57, 57–58
Bellum Italicum (91–88 BC) 70
Bestia, Lucius Calpurnius 11, 46, 47, 86
Bocchus I, King (Mauretania) 6, 11, 69, **75**, 76, 77, 78–79, 80, 81, 82, 89
Bomilcar 11, 55, 57, **58**, **62**, 65
Bonnell, François 16
bribery and corruption 20, 42, 43, 46, 48, 49, 55, 61, 65, 85, 87

Caecilii Metelli 16, **17**, 19–20, 49
Caesar, Gaius Julius 81, **83**, 85, 90
Caesar–Pompeian civil war (49–46 BC) 70
Capsa massacre (107 BC) 74, **74**
Carbo, Cnaeus Papirius 44
Carthage 8, 9, 13, 31, **45**
 destruction of 6, 9, 84
Cato, Caius Porcius 44, 86
Cato the Elder 6, 9, 35, 38
Celts and Celtiberians **15**, 22, 31, **31**, 37, 38, **38**, 53

Cicero 18, 30, 44, 75, 86
Citadel of Vaga 54, 55, 65, 89
client–patron relationships 19, 73
clothing and appearance 21–22, **22**, 33, **36**, **41**
 footwear 30
coin portraits **9**, **13**, **19**, **28**, **48**, **82**
commanders and military discipline and obedience 49–55, **68**, 73, 81
consulships 16, 17, 18, 46, 48, 64, 69–70, 72, 85
Cornelii Scipiones 87
Curio, Scribonius 53

deaths 45, 65, 72
dilectus (selection process) for military service 28–29, 73
Dionysios of Halikarnassos 30
diplomacy and imperialism 43–44, **45**
Djurdjura massif, Algeria 70
domi nobiles (municipal aristocracy) 18
dynastic squabbles 42, 43

elephant hide and shields 23
enrolment and recruitment 72–73
Eutropius 54

First Punic War 31–32
four-ring suspension system 38, **39**
Frontinus 61, 69, 77

Gaetulians 6–8
Galba, Caius Sulpicius 86
Gauda 11, 89
Gisgo, Hasdrubal 9
Gracchus, Caius 73, 86
Gracchus, Tiberius 8
Gulussa, King (Numidia) 12–13, 47, **48**
Gundestrop cauldron 37

helmets 32, 36, **43**, 73
 Boiotian 64
 Etrusco-Corinthian 32, **33**, **41**
 Montefortino **35**
Herodotus 71
Heros (Thracian deity) 53
Hiempsal (son of Micipsa) 11, 15, **16**, 42
Hiempsal II, King (Numidia) 90
Hispania Ulterior 20

imperium and military authority 17
Italian traders in the empire 89–90
Iulii Caesares family 20

Juba I, King (Numidia) 90
Jugurtha 11, **13**, 13–16, **15**, 23, 24, **24**, 25, 42, 43, 44, 45, **45**, 46, 47, 48, 48–49, **54**, 55–56, 57, **59**, 60, 61, **62**, 64–65, **65**, 68, 69, **69**, 70, 71, 73, 74, **75**, 76, 77–81, 82, 84, 85, 86, 87, **88**, 88–89, **89**
 and betrayal of by Bocchus I 78–79, 80, 81, 82
Justinianus, Emperor 54

Laenas, Publius Popillius 86
land distributions for demobilized veterans 72
levies to raise armies 23, 24, 28, 71, 73
lex Claudia (218 BC) 89
Ligurum 76, 77
Limetanus, Caius Mamilius 86
Livy 8, 9, **19**, 21–23, 27, 28, 31, 32, 34, 35, 36, 37, 84
logistics and war doctrine 5
Lucilius 34

Magnus, Pompeius 90
maniples and legions 26–27, 29, 37–38, 40, **40**, 41, 56
mapalia (huts) 8
maps of North Africa and Roman Empire 4, 6, 7, 91
 Numidian theatre of war 47
Marius, Caius 11, 13, **15**, 18, 18–20, 57, 61, 64, 69–70, 71–72, 73–74, **74**, 75, 75–76, 77, **77**, 81, 82, 85, **85**, 89, 89
Martial 84
Masaesyli Numidians 8–9
Masinissa, King (Numidia) 8, 9, **9**, **10**, 12, **19**, 21, 25, 42, 48, 76
massacre of Italians at Cirta 45–46, 82
Massiva (son of Gulussa) 47–48, **48**, 65
Massylii Numidians 8
Mastanabal, King (Numidia) 12–13, 48
Mauretania 6, **60**, 75, 90
Mauretanian horsemen **21**, 77
Mausoleum Soumaa d'el-Khroub, Algeria 16, **25**, **27**, 29
Memmius, Caius 85, 86
Metellus, Quintus Caecilius 11, 16, **17**, 20, 49, **54**, 54–55, 56, 57, 58, 59, 60, 61, **62**, 64, 65, 65–69, **68**, 69, 70–72, 73–74, 81, 82, 85
Micipsa, King (Numidia) 11, **12**, 13, 15, **16**, **19**, 42, 48
military experience 17–18, 30, 54, 73
military strengths and complements 29
Milo, Titus Annius 83

Monument of Aemilius Paullus 34
Muluccha (Moulouya) river 75, 75–76, 90

nobilitas (hereditary aristocracy) 18, 44, 47, 70, 71, 85, 86, 87
novi homines 18, **85**
   divisions with *nobiles* 70, 71, 82, 85
Numantia hill fort **15**
Numidia and the Numidians 5, 8–10, **10**, 21–22, 74–75, 89
   partitions of 86, 90
Numidian army 9, 13, 24, **24**, 29, 49, 58–59, 61, **66–67, 68**, 73
Numidian horses and horsemen **19**, 21, **21**, **22**, 22–23, **23**, 24, **24**, 25, 36, 65, **66–67, 68**
Numidian monument **12**
Numidian tactics and strategy 23, 24–25, 28, 44, 47, 48–49, 55–56, 57–60, **59**, 63, 64–65, **65**, 68, 70, 71, 76, 77, 82
Numidian war elephants 28, **60**, 61

Opimius, Lucius 11, 86

Paterculus, Velleius 71–72
patronage and electoral bribery 20
peace negotiations 46
peoples and tribes of north Africa 6–9, 61
phalanx formations 26–27, 40
Phoenicians 43
physical endurance in hand-to-hand combat 39, 40
Picq, Col Ardent du 40
plebeian tribunes 16, 20, **83**, 86
Pliny the Elder 8, 9
Plutarch 19, 82, 88, **89**
political ambition and power struggles 70, 72, 85, 87
Polybios 6, 8, 21, 27, 28, 29, 30, 31, 32, 33, 34, 35, 36, 37, 38, 39, 40, **73**, 84
Pompeius Aulus, Quintus 19
Principate 21, **21**, 33, 39
principle of collegiality 16
property qualification for enlistment 72
propraetor (provincial governor) 20
provincia Africa and Roman governance 6
Punic silver double shekel coin **28**
puppet rulers and alliances 6

quaestio Mamiliana 86–87
Quintilianus 84

Regulus, Marcus Atilius 5
Roman Army 5, 15, 24, 25–27, 28–30, **50–51**, 52, 54, 56, 58–59, 60–61, **62**, **66–67, 68**
   auxiliaries
      Mauretanian horsemen **21**
      Numidian horsemen 21, **21**, 65
      Thracian horsemen **53**
   equites (cavalry) 34–37, 60, 61, **64**, 80
      equites equo publico (equestrian elite) 35
   hastati (young spearmen) 29, 37, 38, 39
   legions 29, 30–31, **34**, 40, **40**, 61, 72
      legio III 49, **52**, 61, **62**
      Polybian legionaries 29, 30–33, **64**
   principes (chief men) 39
   triarii (veteran third-rank men) 39–40, **40**
   velites (light infantry) 29, 33–34, 37, 38, **64**, **73**
Roman assault on fortress near Muluccha river 75, **75**, 76–77
Roman constitution 16
Roman padded saddle 36–37
Roman Republic 70, 85
Roman strategy and tactics 5, 11, 37–41, 43–44, 46–47, 48, 49, **54**, 56–57, 60, **62**, 64, 65–69, **69**, 71, 72, 73–77, 81, 82, 89, 90
Rufus, Publius Rutilius 57, **57**, 60, **62**, 64

Sallust (Caius Sallustius Crispus) 8, **8**, 11, 13, **13**, 15, 18, 23, 42, 43–44, 45, 46, **47**, 48, 49, 54, 57, 60, 61–64, 70, 71, 74, 75, **75**, 76, 77, **83**, 86, 88, **88**, 89, 90, **90**
   Bellum Catilinae (monograph) 83
   Bellum Iugurthinum (monograph) 84, **84**, 87
   on the Roman Republic and geopolitics 83–85, 87
Scaurus, Marcus Aemilius 11, 44, 46, 86
Scipio Aemilianus, Publius Cornelius 5, 13, 15, **15**, 16, 19, 42, 55
Scipiones 16
Scordisci 44, 46
Second Punic War (218–201 BC) 6, 8, 9, 27, 38, **45**
Seleukid thorakites 27
Senate 15, 17, 42, 43, 44, 45, 46, 47, 48, 49, 69, 73, **83**, 84, 85–86, 87, 89, 90
senatorial generals 17–18, 85, 87
Senonian Gauls 35
siege of Cirta, Algeria (112 BC) 44–45, **45**

siege of Numantia (134–133 BC) 13–15, **14**, **15**, 19, 31
siege of Suthul (110 BC) 48, **52**
siege of Thala (108 BC) 11, 69, **69**, 71, 74
siege of Zama (109 BC) 64–65, **65**
Sittius, Publius 90
Sophonisba 9
Statorius, Quintus 9
Stele d'Abizar **24**
Strabo 9, 21, 23, **23**
Sulla, Lucius Cornelius 11, 77, **77**, **78–79**, 80, 81, 82, **82**, 85
Sulla–Marian civil war (88–82 BC) 70, **82**, 85
supplies 74
Syme 87
Syphax 9, 25

Table de Jugurtha mesa, Tunisia 76
Tacitus 39
Third Macedonian War (171–168 BC) 53
Third Samnite War (298–290 BC) 31
Thracian army 24, 44, 46, 49, **52**, **53**, 65
Tiepolo, Giovanni Battista
   Trionfo di Mario (painting) **89**
training and gladiatorial schools 64
Trajan's Column, Rome 21, **22**
trench foot 30
triplex acies battle formation 37–38, 56, **58**
Triumvir–Liberator civil war (42 BC) 70
Tullianum (Carcere Mamertino) **88**
turmae (cavalry units) 34–35

Vegetius 5, 30, 39
Vermina 9

war booty **26**, 64, 71–72, 74, **74**, 89
war doctrine and theory 5, 40–41
   and the ambush 63, **66–67, 68**
war indemnity payments 46, 85
weaponry 23, 24, **24**, 27, 30, 32, 36, **41**
   spears and javelins 29, 30, 33, 34, **36**, **66–67, 68**
      hasta spear 30, **40**
      pilum 30, 31–32, 38, 39
   swords 38–39
      Delos sword 39
      falcata sword 32
      gladius Hispaniensis 31, 31–32, 33, 36, **38**, 39, 40
      iron sword 25, 31
Wolfe, James 46

yoke 49